# Going Beyond Loaning Books to Loaning Technologies

## About the Series

This innovative series written and edited for librarians by librarians provides authoritative, practical information and guidance on a wide spectrum of library processes and operations.

Books in the series are focused, describing practical and innovative solutions to a problem facing today's librarian and delivering step-by-step guidance for planning, creating, implementing, managing, and evaluating a wide range of services and programs.

The books are aimed at beginning and intermediate librarians needing basic instruction/guidance in a specific subject and at experienced librarians who need to gain knowledge in a new area or guidance in implementing a new program/service.

## About the Series Editor

The **Practical Guides for Librarians** series was conceived by and is edited by M. Sandra Wood, MLS, MBA, AHIP, FMLA, Librarian Emerita, Penn State University Libraries.

M. Sandra Wood was a librarian at the George T. Harrell Library, The Milton S. Hershey Medical Center, College of Medicine, Pennsylvania State University, Hershey, PA, for over 35 years, specializing in reference, educational, and database services. Ms. Wood worked for several years as a Development Editor for Neal-Schuman Publishers.

Ms. Wood received a MLS from Indiana University and a MBA from the University of Maryland. She is a Fellow of the Medical Library Association and served as a member of MLA's Board of Directors from 1991 to 1995. Ms. Wood is founding and current editor of *Medical Reference Services Quarterly*, now in its 35th volume. She also was founding editor of the *Journal of Consumer Health on the Internet* and the *Journal of Electronic Resources in Medical Libraries* and served as editor/co-editor of both journals through 2011.

## Titles in the Series

1. *How to Teach: A Practical Guide for Librarians* by Beverley E. Crane
2. *Implementing an Inclusive Staffing Model for Today's Reference Services* by Julia K. Nims, Paula Storm, and Robert Stevens
3. *Managing Digital Audiovisual Resources: A Practical Guide for Librarians* by Matthew C. Mariner
4. *Outsourcing Technology: A Practical Guide for Librarians* by Robin Hastings
5. *Making the Library Accessible for All: A Practical Guide for Librarians by* Jane Vincent
6. *Discovering and Using Historical Geographical Resources on the Web: A Practical Guide for Librarians* by Eva H. Dodsworth and L. W. Laliberté
7. *Digitization and Digital Archiving: A Practical Guide for Librarians* by Elizabeth R. Leggett
8. *Makerspaces: A Practical Guide for Librarians* by John J. Burke
9. *Implementing Web-Scale Discovery Services: A Practical Guide for Librarians* by JoLinda Thompson
10. *Using iPhones and iPads: A Practical Guide for Librarians* by Matthew Connolly and Tony Cosgrave
11. *Usability Testing: A Practical Guide for Librarians* by Rebecca Blakiston
12. *Mobile Devices: A Practical Guide for Librarians* by Ben Rawlins
13. *Going Beyond Loaning Books to Loaning Technologies: A Practical Guide for Librarians* by Janelle Sander, Lori S. Mestre, and Eric Kurt

# Going Beyond Loaning Books to Loaning Technologies

## A Practical Guide for Librarians

**Janelle Sander**
**Lori S. Mestre**
**Eric Kurt**

PRACTICAL GUIDES FOR LIBRARIANS, NO. 13

ROWMAN & LITTLEFIELD
*Lanham • Boulder • New York • London*

Published by Rowman & Littlefield
A wholly owned subsidiary of The Rowman & Littlefield Publishing Group, Inc.
4501 Forbes Boulevard, Suite 200, Lanham, Maryland 20706
www.rowman.com

Unit A, Whitacre Mews, 26-34 Stannary Street, London SE11 4AB



British Library Cataloguing in Publication Information Available

**Library of Congress Cataloging-in-Publication Data**

Sander, Janelle, 1982–, author.
Going beyond loaning books to loaning technologies : a practical guide for librarians / Janelle Sander, Lori S. Mestre, Eric Kurt.
pages cm. — (Practical guides for librarians ; 13)
Includes bibliographical references and index.
ISBN 978-1-4422-4499-3 (pbk. : alk. paper) — ISBN 978-1-4422-4500-6 (ebook)
1. Library circulation and loans. 2. Multimedia library services. 3. Libraries—Special collections—Audio-visual equipment. 4. Libraries—Special collections—Nonbook materials. I. Mestre, Lori, author. II. Kurt, Eric, 1979–, author. III. Title.
Z712.S36 2015
025.6—dc23 2014034572

∞™ The paper used in this publication meets the minimum requirements of American National Standard for Information Sciences—Permanence of Paper for Printed Library Materials, ANSI/NISO Z39.48-1992.

Printed in the United States of America

To the staff of the Undergraduate Library at the University of Illinois at Urbana-Champaign.
Their patience, flexibility, openness to innovation, and feedback make it possible
to have a successful loanable technology program.

# Contents

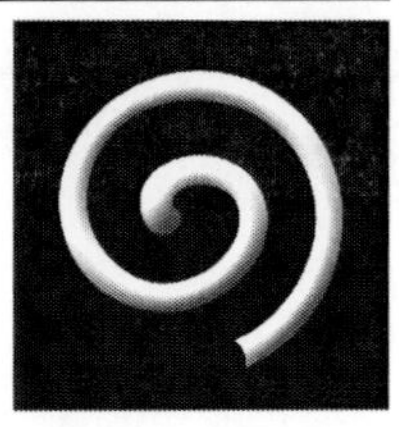

# List of Figures and Tables

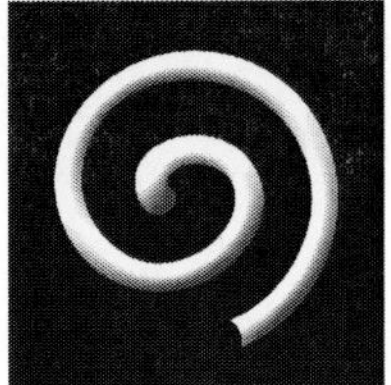

## Figures

## Tables

# Preface

*Going Beyond Loaning Books to Loaning Technologies: A Practical Guide for Librarians* covers the process and pipeline of establishing and maintaining an effective loanable technology program. Included are guidelines, suggestions, and examples of developing and maintaining a loanable technology program that supports multiple constituencies, including at school, public, and academic libraries. Many of the examples and suggestions provided here are based on creating and expanding a loanable technology program at the Undergraduate Library at the University of Illinois at Urbana-Champaign (UIUC). Although all the challenges, successes, and recommendations cannot be fully shared here, some of the key themes that will be further discussed throughout the book include processes and suggestions for selection, processing, cataloging, circulation, maintenance, and promotion of the equipment and services in the program. Chapters contain step-by-step information, complete with forms, templates, and examples that cover all aspects of developing, implementing, and maintaining a loanable technology program. More detailed information pertaining to the development and stages of the UIUC loanable technology program can be found in appendix A.

While many of the examples in *Going Beyond Loaning Books to Loaning Technologies: A Practical Guide for Librarians* are based on this program, they are presented in ways that are generic enough for implementation by all types of libraries. Additional examples from other library types are also included in the chapters. Providing loanable technology that can be borrowed by library patrons is a continuously expanding service at many libraries, especially as faculty and teachers require multimodal projects. For some libraries, loanable technology might include calculators, gaming devices, headphones, e-readers, laptops, and tablets. Increasingly, though, there is also demand for all types of cameras, lighting, voice recorders, microphones, external storage devices, projectors, peripherals, and converters, among hundreds of possibilities. This guide provides the nuts and bolts and the "behind-the-scenes" details of developing a program and walks librarians and information technology professionals through even some of the complex decisions and processes, such as:

- needs assessment
- budget allocation
- selecting, cataloging, processing, and storing equipment

- circulation, billing, and troubleshooting
- training
- collaborating with others to offer consultation services
- promoting the service
- assessment

## Organization of This Book

*Going Beyond Loaning Books to Loaning Technologies: A Practical Guide for Librarians* is divided into eleven chapters. Each chapter covers a practical aspect related to developing and maintaining a loanable technology program, including many illustrations. As previously mentioned, appendix A contains the background for how the program at UIUC was established, including its stages. Chapters 1 through 4 provide the background needed to strategically develop a program, including garnering support, determining need, creating a plan, selecting equipment, and setting a budget. Chapters 5 through 9 detail the behind-the-scenes operations to catalog, process, package, and house items; to develop policies and procedures, including the checkout and check-in processes; and to navigate billing operations. The last two chapters provide suggestions for training programs and assessment. Two appendixes contain additional examples related to assessment and the UIUC program.

Chapter 1 articulates some of the key factors related to establishing a program, such as garnering support from the community of users, connecting the program to your library's mission, vision, and strategic-planning documents, and some initial determinants for selecting loanable technology. These determinants—perceived need, functionality, practicality, and cost—are used as a basis for designing a needs assessment, which is covered in chapter 2. It describes the process for creating a technology plan and steps for conducting a needs assessment. Once you have analyzed the results of the needs assessment, you will need to convene stakeholders (or an advisory group) to help in the appropriate selection of equipment to purchase.

Chapter 3 provides suggestions for this process, as well as steps for developing a loanable technology collection, including steps for the planning process, strategies to determine types of basic and high-end equipment to purchase, and considerations for deciding whether items will circulate only within the library or can be used outside of the library. Although the budget is mentioned in chapter 3, a more comprehensive conversation of determining a budget can be found in chapter 4. Planning a budget for a loanable technology program can have multiple stages built in, including initial costs for a program and ongoing costs. This chapter includes suggestions for start-up costs and ongoing costs for equipment, equipment storage, file storage, packaging for equipment, supplies, repair, and peripherals. Also discussed are possible budget streams.

Chapter 5 discusses options for cataloging equipment, including types of cataloging formats, records, and best practices for cataloging loanable technology. This chapter includes specific details, as well as screenshots, for establishing parameters for loan periods and renewal options, and creating MARC bibliographic, holdings, and item records as well as serial holdings records. Because there is much more involved in the whole process of obtaining, inventorying, cataloging, processing, and preparing loanable technology items than for a single monograph, special attention is given, in chapter 6, to steps for processing, packaging, and housing the equipment. Along with suggested steps to inventory, process, package, and label the equipment, examples of equipment-loan forms, templates, and web pages are also included. Chapter 7 includes examples of the policies needed to manage a loanable technology program. Types of policies that are covered are: collection development; use of items; borrowing privileges; loan periods; renewals; reservation of items; lost, stolen, or unreturned items; and privacy and confidentiality.

In chapter 8, you will learn options for developing equipment-loan forms, reserving and renewing equipment, preparing technology to be checked out, creating a check-in process, preparing items to recirculate, and developing patron equipment-problem forms (if items are damaged or parts are missing). Because there are inevitably instances when items are lost, broken, or not returned, library staff will need to contact patrons. Chapter 9 discusses how to handle billing issues, including both patron-initiated contact with the library and library-initiated contact with the patron. Included are questions to ask to help determine billing practices and tips for templates and scripts that can be used.

Training to use the equipment, both by staff and patrons, should be a part of your loanable technology program. Chapter 10 contains suggestions for staff training, as well as options for educating patrons on the care and use of the equipment. Included are examples for group trainings, in-space workshops, on-location workshops, consultations, tours, and guides and demonstrations for using the equipment. The last chapter circles back to assessment, which is initially covered in chapter 2 (needs assessment). Whereas chapter 2 provides ideas for gathering information to help with the initial start of a program, chapter 11 goes into much more detail about types of quantitative and qualitative methods that can be used to assess the program. It provides ideas that can be used to gather patron feedback on use patterns, needs, gaps, success stories, and suggestions for improving the program. Appendix B provides additional examples of surveys.

Practical and easy to understand, *Going Beyond Loaning Books to Loaning Technologies: A Practical Guide for Librarians* offers the complete package for anyone interested in lending technology to patrons.

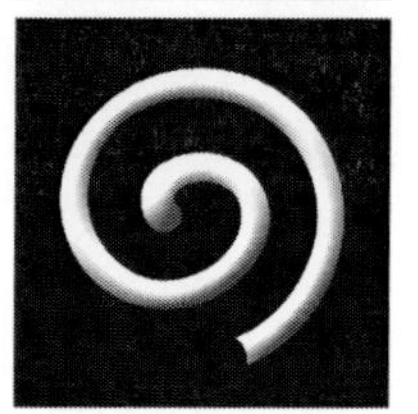

# Acknowledgments

We would like to express our appreciation and thanks to M. Sandra Wood, series editor, who has done an outstanding job in her editing skills for the manuscript and in her work shepherding this book. Her prompt and helpful attention was unexpected and was also very educational.

Janelle would like to thank God for his grace in her life and her husband, Jeremiah, for his unwavering support and encouragement. Lori would like to acknowledge the many individuals who have donated funds to the Undergraduate Library at the University of Illinois at Urbana-Champaign. It is mainly through those donations that we have been able to provide the loanable technology that makes this extraordinary service available to our constituents. Eric would like to thank Elizabeth for her consistent love and support, and Emma for her never-ceasing joy and curiosity.

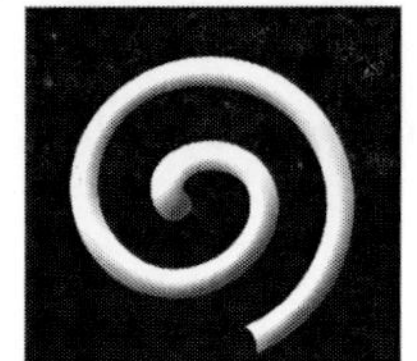

# CHAPTER 1

# Establishing a Loanable Technology Program

**IN THIS CHAPTER**

- ▷ How loanable technology programs benefit library communities
- ▷ The value of garnering support from the campus/community
- ▷ The importance of connecting your loanable technology program to your library's mission, vision, and strategic-planning documents
- ▷ Some initial criteria to help guide a loanable technology program

## How Loanable Technology Programs Benefit Library Communities

TODAY'S STUDENTS AND library patrons have an increasing need for equipment that will allow them to complete projects that incorporate multimedia. Students in high schools and colleges have generational experiences and expectations that differ significantly from prior populations. These students require a range of digital tools that are configurable for immediate needs and hold the most relevance to the digital world they inhabit. They are often required to create projects in a format other than as a text document. Likewise, faculty increasingly expect multimodal projects that incorporate students' research. Schoolteachers and librarians at the K–12 levels need to address how they are meeting the technology standards, which include requirements for competency in technology and in becoming technologically literate. In addition to state requirements, some of the national standards include: the American Association of School Librarians' "Standards for the 21st Century Learner," http://ala.org/ala/mgrps/divs/aasl/guidelinesandstandards/learningstandards/AASL_LearningStandards.pdf; the International Society for Technology in Education standards, http://www.iste.org/standards; the Common Core Standards, http://www.corestandards.org/; and the United States Department of Education's National Education Technology

Plan, http://www.ed.gov/technology/netp-2010, which requires that educators not only know and understand the standards but can demonstrate how to integrate technology and embed technology tools and applications into the classroom for teaching and learning. Teacher-librarians in both public- and independent-school settings are enabling students to move beyond the classroom walls as they assist teachers and students in adopting mobile technology, laptops, tablets, and multimedia. Multimedia can be used to augment projects, blogs, websites, and assignments, and teachers can serve as role models for using multimedia and in encouraging students in their use.

Whether in schools, public libraries, colleges, or universities, it is rarely feasible for each department to acquire all the technology needed to support multimedia efforts or to require that each student purchase the equipment. Libraries are uniquely situated to meet this expanded need for tools to aid content creation, in addition to content retrieval and consumption through programs that purchase and loan out digital-use devices and other technology. This also applies to the general population, which could benefit from access to the types of technologies available for work, recreational, or personal projects.

## Importance of Garnering Support from Stakeholders

For the loanable technology program to be a success, it is important to look outside the department establishing the loanable technology program and its staff for expertise and support. There is a wealth of benefits that can be gained from communicating to others early on regarding the planning and strategy of a loanable technology endeavor.

Each external group consulted can bring its own level of expertise and assistance. In the case of academic libraries some obvious groups may be faculty and staff, while potentially less obvious groups might be departmental or central information technology services, as well as other media-creation services. For public libraries it will be important to work with the Board of Trustees, the Friends group, local schools, and community members. Stakeholders for schools should include administrators, specialists, teachers, students, parents, and community members.

Most often, the greatest hurdle in working with the various groups lies in the initial contact and establishment of a first meeting. Once contact has been made, buy-in is usually simple, since most groups tend toward collaboration, as long as a heavy physical or time-based burden is not placed upon them. For example, to create and expand the loanable technology program at the University of Illinois, groups contacted were more than willing to offer opinions and information when asked what types of equipment hardware and software they would like to see in a loanable technology initiative. This is especially true if the resources will, in turn, directly benefit the groups consulted, which they often will. Media-creation and technology-centric departments are excellent resources for outside research and advice on specific models or categories of equipment to purchase. Faculty and staff (or students, parents, and teachers) will be able to offer suggestions and viewpoints on what their current needs are for class-specific projects and educational enhancement. Students can offer a unique opinion on what they see as beneficial for their study and progress throughout their programs. All these different viewpoints, while unique, offer viable information for the success of a loanable technology program. Chapter 11 will provide additional suggestions for developing partners for a program.

## Initial Aspects for Selecting Loanable Technology

In order to develop a sustainable loanable technology program that meets the needs of your constituency, requests for equipment need to be evaluated and prioritized for acquisition (regardless of how far outside the box they may seem at first). For example, criteria might be prioritized as follows:

- compliance with loanable technology mission
- perceived need
- functionality
- practicality
- cost

### Compliance with a Loanable Technology Mission

First and foremost, technology that the library purchases should be in line with the mission for the library's loanable technology program, which should be part of the library's vision and mission statements. The loanable technology program mission should include statements about providing and supporting technology, which you can then use as a guide whenever you consider adding new items to your loanable technology pool. In this way, developing a loanable technology pool is very similar to establishing pools for items such as books and media, which are also subject to the vision and mission statement of the library. Further discussion of the vision and mission follows this section.

### Perceived Need

Chapter 2 provides guidelines and suggestions for conducting a needs assessment to determine the types of equipment to purchase. Most of the activities to be implemented from the needs assessment will (or should) be directed toward meeting identified needs. Once you have established the need for a loanable technology program and garnered the necessary support from your campus, school, or community, you will probably start receiving requests for additional equipment items to have available for circulation. Commonly requested technology usually falls into one of two categories: items that would make a user's stay in a library more convenient, and items that are too expensive for the average person to purchase. Usually, items requested in the first category are items that would typically stay in the library (chargers, headphones, USB cables, laptops, etc.), and items in the second category are those that would be allowed to leave the library (cameras, handheld gaming equipment, tablets, voice recorders, projectors, speakers, etc.).

Measuring perceived need includes both listening to requests and monitoring the status of items already circulating. Patrons who learn that a library has some equipment they can borrow may also ask if other equipment might be available. Being attentive to verbal requests is a great way to discover patron needs instead of assuming need. More about conducting a needs assessment will be discussed in chapter 2.

Monitoring items that are already circulating can indicate when more copies of an item are needed. For example, are the laptop or phone chargers checked out so frequently that there is a constant waiting list? Are the projectors all booked in advance for two months? These could be signals that a few more copies might be needed. Of course, new items and new copies of items need to adhere to your established loanable technology collection development policy, which might include a cap on the number of copies of any given type of equipment.

It is important that users have both formal and informal avenues to request new technology. Formal requests might include online or paper surveys, web forms, or e-mails. Informal requests are received through conversations or brainstorming sessions.

### Functionality

What function or theoretical usefulness will the new item serve? For instance, in an academic setting, if students need to complete a class project for which they are required to shoot video, having video cameras available for circulation fills a functional need (provided that supporting class projects is part of the mission of the loanable tech program). However, an important consideration is to determine what type of camera (or equipment) will most efficiently fulfill that function. Conversations with faculty, teachers, parents, patrons, or students and a review of resources are important steps in this process. More information on this can be found in chapter 3.

### Practicality

Practicality relates to the pragmatic usefulness of the item. If, for example, you have determined that video cameras will be part of the loanable tech pool, then practicality becomes the step in which the pros and cons of different brands and models must be evaluated. Included in this step is an analysis of the user-friendliness or usability of the item, in addition to an assessment of professional and user reviews to gain an informed perspective. This topic is discussed in more depth in chapter 3.

### Cost

Finally, cost should be considered. Cost and budget will almost certainly be discussed early in the evaluation process, but in some cases cost could be the final determining factor in whether or not to purchase an item. Choices may need to be considered as to how much money you can allot to this purchase and how many copies you can have for circulation. If you are fortunate, there will be a budget line for technology support and replacement costs, but if not, other choices may need to be made. Chapter 3 provides options when considering the purchase of an item, and chapter 4 provides an overview of budget considerations.

## Vision for a Loanable Technology Program: Library Side

Librarians and those working in libraries know the importance of aligning services with the vision and mission of the library or the strategic plan (which should be closely in line with the larger institution's vision and mission or strategic plan). Often the administration will fund or promote services only if they are supporting the vision, mission, and strategic initiatives of the library or institution. When you develop your vision and goals for your library, look for statements from the library plan that discuss "information technologies," "innovative services," or similar ideas, and use those phrases in your vision statement (but expand on them). Following are some examples of phrases that might be in a strategic plan or mission statement that could be copied into a specific loanable technology mission or vision statement. Look at what your library has already included and then create your document using some of the same phrases. It may be necessary for you to further describe how each phrase or bullet applies to loanable technology and modify as needed. Some examples follow:

- design and deliver exceptional user services
- identify and apply new information technologies
- stimulate innovation in library practices, services, and technologies
- support teaching and learning programs
- design and implement a service program as a campus-wide resource for media-literacy education, course-integrated media-content creation and evaluation, and curation of student-created media content
- design and implement a collaboration, consultation, and instructional space that provides instructional and scholarly support services to undergraduate researchers, graduate students, and faculty

Beginning with the library strategic plan, you can then revise your mission and vision statements to align with the plan, while focusing more on the innovation and technology aspect. If the mission and vision statements of your library need to be updated, add elements that support the value of a loanable technology program. You might include some of these phrases to represent the loanable technology program:

- foster and promote an inviting, innovative, and evolving educational environment
- provide academic, co-curricular, cultural, and technological support to our users and become a dynamic, innovative unit
- engage patrons in the inquiry process and educate them in their roles as content consumers and creators in the design, production, and delivery of content and media for research, discovery, and learning
- promote critical thinking skills and information, technology, and media literacy
- provide expertise in identifying, interpreting, and utilizing appropriate credible and scholarly information resources, course materials, technology, media, and materials for personal or recreational consumption
- increase availability of curriculum-based information resources to increase student, staff, and teacher efforts in presentations and projects by acquiring audio and video multimedia equipment, laptops, scanners, VHS/DVD/Blu-ray players, tablets, personal digital assistants (PDAs), chargers, input devices and output devices, peripherals, and tools that provide the user with access from any place in the library to library resources and the Internet
- investigate and implement new and emerging technologies
- provide facilities, services, and technology in a predictable, safe, and dependable manner

Although a loanable technology program has many benefits for students, staff, educators, and community members, it involves a lot of preplanning and continual evaluation to keep it current and relevant. Developing a loanable technology program has significant effects on a variety of library public and technical services, including a library's space use and allocation, cataloging, processing, and staff training. These can be beneficial, yet challenging. This book provides guidance on addressing the challenges of a loanable technology program and setting one up so that it can be successful and sustainable.

## Key Points

A loanable technology program at a library can benefit the community in many ways but requires a lot of planning and collaboration among stakeholders. Following are some of the ideas expressed in this chapter:

- A centralized library location is the optimal place for housing a loanable technology program that will support teachers and faculty as they incorporate and integrate technologies into the classroom. The program also assists students and patrons who are required to (or wish to) create projects using multimedia.
- For the loanable technology program to be a success it is important to look outside the department establishing the loanable technology program and its staff for expertise and support.
- Criteria to evaluate technology for a program include addressing compliance with a loanable technology mission, perceived need, functionality, practicality, and cost.
- The library purchases should be in line with the vision and mission statements for the overall library's loanable technology program.

The next chapter will describe the process for creating a technology plan and steps for conducting a needs assessment that will help in determining many aspects of your program.

CHAPTER 2

# Identifying Need

**IN THIS CHAPTER**

- ▷ The value and steps of creating and implementing a loanable technology plan
- ▷ The importance of conducting periodic needs assessments for a loanable technology program
- ▷ Examples of types of assessment
- ▷ Suggestions for administering the assessment and analyzing the data

DETERMINING NEED AND gathering evidence for the development of a loanable technology program can have multiple stages. Included in this chapter are suggestions and examples for an initial needs assessment, developing a technology plan, types of assessment to consider, administering the assessment, and analyzing the data. Other chapters will discuss budgeting for a loanable technology program as well as cataloging, processing, managing, and publicizing the program, which should all be taken into consideration when considering whether to initiate a new program or grow an existing program.

## Initial Thoughts for Conducting a Needs Assessment

It is not unusual for libraries to provide various equipment and peripherals for patron use based on frequent questions regarding availability. These may have begun as queries from patrons about whether the library had a calculator, USB drive, phone charger, or certain cables to connect their device to a computer so they could transfer multimedia. Initially, if these items were purchased, they may have been handled as in-house circulation efforts and not officially catalogued. However, once the collection of items grows beyond consumable items and patrons begin to expect that the library will have these and other items, the library should conduct an official needs assessment to determine types of items and quantities to have in stock as part of a loanable technology program.

In the case of school libraries and certain public and academic libraries, an important justification for need may be that there are technology mandates and standards in place. Seek out the standards and guidelines for what is expected in your community or state and what will be assessed, if part of a school accrediting agency, in regards to programming and training. These may help inform the type of needs assessment that you plan to conduct. What will be provided in this chapter are steps for determining the needs of your library and environment.

Before determining whether to buy equipment, you should have a plan for using the technology. A needs assessment will help in the evaluation of the types of equipment that are necessary in order to satisfy requirements (for your mission or vision, class needs, campus needs, or community needs). In your vision for a technology program, it is also important to consider the necessary resources, including staff, training, and management policies, that will be required to fulfill this vision. The initial assessment will help evaluate what you currently provide, gaps in what is provided, and the preferred services and offerings. These could all be documented in a technology plan. Although some libraries may conduct a needs assessment before developing a loanable technology plan, others may draft a technology plan based on the directions and goals of the library. A loanable technology plan can also help identify the strengths and weaknesses of a program. The next section will discuss the benefit of creating a loanable technology plan, followed by the section on needs assessment.

## Loanable Technology Plan

The loanable technology plan is included in this part of the chapter because some of the same components and framework for creating a plan are directly intertwined with the work done for a needs assessment. The library may already have a technology plan that focuses on information technology and infrastructure, but it may not mention the vision or goals for acquiring and managing loanable equipment or peripherals. Some institutions may feel these items fall under collections, and, indeed, a collection development policy for loanable technology is also needed and is further discussed in chapters 3 and 7. A technology plan should detail what resources, equipment, and services already exist and what goals the library has for the future. The plan will provide short-term and long-term planning. The plan should also supplement and support the library's strategic plan. A separate loanable technology plan provides the library with a mechanism to explain, in detail, the technology initiatives to be undertaken to meet identified needs. Although a library strategic plan may be updated every three to five years, a separate loanable technology plan may need to be reviewed more often because of the constant advances in technology.

A technology plan can help determine the collective needs of a library and of staff, as related to the use of technology in educational settings, and can be used to support teaching and learning activities for both staff and students. It should include information to help planners—administrators, technology and media specialists, and school or technology planning-team members. It can be used to make purchasing, resource-allocation, or other decisions relating to technology. This plan could also indicate the potential effects of technology on teaching practice and student outcomes or on public-engagement efforts for community members and can also be used for professional development for staff and educators. Please see textbox 2.1 for some examples of technology plans. Additionally, for a good overview of creating a technology plan see Cohn and Kelsey (2009) and Dugan (2002).

**TEXTBOX 2.1**

Following are some examples of technology plans, although most technology plans only briefly include handheld items or multimedia equipment.

- Eden Prairie Schools Technology Plan, 2012–2015: https://webmedia.edenpr.org/District/Documents/technology_plan_2012-2015.pdf
- Nome Public Schools Technology Plan, 2013–2016: http://www.nomeschools.com/documents/NPS_Technology_Plan1316.pdf
- Saint Paul Public Schools Technology Plan, 2013–2015: http://bit.ly/1hwl7Eh

## Benefits of a Loanable Technology Plan

A library may not need to create a loanable technology plan until the program has grown beyond simply loaning out a few items and until a needs assessment has made it clearer what types of equipment are needed. As a program evolves, the need for an organized plan, including goals and priorities, becomes increasingly important, especially if budget increases are desired. Creation of a loanable technology plan can be time consuming. Some of the reasons for creating a plan are to:

- identify weaknesses and strengths concerning technological implementations;
- determine a vision and strategic directions;
- identify and prioritize needed technologies to support teaching, learning, research needs, and library services and programs;
- help organize technology implementation, such as introducing new technologies and migrating to updated hardware versions or software releases;
- inform everyone concerned (users, staff, and administrators) of what the library is doing;
- manage budgeting and expenditures, helping to reduce the chances of unplanned liabilities and acquisitions;
- aid in creating a development or fundraising plan, which could be especially useful if a donor should drop by wanting to provide an "unplanned" gift; and
- measure, evaluate, and assess progress by helping to answer accountability questions—are the technologies effectively applied to meet the educational mission of the library (such as increased information competencies), and are service operations improved through increased efficiencies and productivity?

## Creating the Loanable Technology Plan

Following are suggested steps for creating a loanable technology plan.

1. Convene a planning committee. A planning committee will need to determine the extent of what should be in a plan based on the library community and intended use. Creating a plan is a participatory process. Involve as many of the players and end users as possible, including library staff, faculty, students, administrative and

academic computing staff, and other library users and advocates, such as the library's alumni group, or a local friends of the library group.

2. Articulate an agreed-to process to develop the plan. Determine a time frame for plan-development activities, such as meeting dates and progress milestones (i.e., stipulate that the first draft of the plan will be completed by a specific date).
3. Determine the needs of the various end users and other stakeholders. This step is critical. Although the planning committee may be confident that they know these needs, insist on querying the stakeholders and end users. Satisfaction surveys may help identify broad needs. Focus groups would help refine those needs, and the questioning process may yield valuable insights that will be helpful when prioritizing implementation activities later.
4. Articulate the findings of the needs assessment and develop appropriate documents, such as service-based vision and mission statements. A vision is a statement of what the library wants to become; a mission statement, another piece of the library's overall plan, discusses what the library is or does.
5. Determine goals and objectives, budget, and priorities. The goals and objectives should relate to services and service-related applications. The budget should determine costs and align the plan with the budget year. Priorities can then be established by year, depending on goals for each year and budget allocation.

Textbox 2.2 suggests some websites with templates to guide you through the process of creating a technology plan.

### TEXTBOX 2.2

### TECHNOLOGY PLAN TEMPLATES

- OCLC Web Junction has resources to assist with the development of a library technology plan: http://www.webjunction.org/explore-topics/tech-planning.html
- The Minnesota Department of Education provides a template for a technology plan and some needs assessment tools: http://education.state.mn.us/MDE/SchSup/SchTech/
- National Center for Education Statistics: http://nces.ed.gov/pubs2005/tech_suite/part_1.asp#3

Once costs are determined and priorities are established, an implementation plan is drawn up. This includes details of what is going to be done, when, and how much of what resources will be required. Examples of resources include funding, training for staff and users, and additional electrical needs, including electrical hookups within tables and chairs. However, in order to get to that point, it is first necessary to conduct a needs assessment.

## Conducting a Needs Assessment

A technology plan provides the roadmap for the program, but it is also important to learn the actual needs for the program, which can be based on many variables. As mentioned

## TEXTBOX 2.3

### WEBSITES WITH NEEDS ASSESSMENT DOCUMENTS

From Web Junction:

- http://www.webjunction.org/explore-topics/needs-assessment.html
- http://www.webjunction.org/documents/webjunction/Technology_Needs_Assessment.html

From the National Center for Education Statistics' Forum Unified Education Technology Suite:

- http://nces.ed.gov/pubs2005/tech_suite/

above, some libraries may decide to do a needs assessment before creating the technology plan. Needs assessments can help identify gaps in services, priorities for a program or service, problems and possible solutions, and growth opportunities. Textbox 2.3 provides some websites that have examples of needs assessment documents.

When planning for a needs assessment, you will need to determine answers to some questions before moving forward. For example: Who conducts the study? What kind of information will be collected? How will the information be collected? How will the results be analyzed and disseminated? These questions are explored further below.

**Who conducts the study?** It is important to consider who will conduct the study. Often it is advisable to use individuals who are not part of the organization so they will not be "biased" or provide leading questions. However, with good planning and training the facilitators could be:

- outside consultants
- volunteers from the community
- library staff

**What kind of information will be collected?** Think about what you want to know. What will help you make decisions about the services, programs, and training to offer? The information you collect might include:

- current technology being used (also when individuals most often need the equipment, e.g., weekends, long holidays, particular times of the semester)
- purposes for using the technology (classes, projects, recreational, etc.) and for how long
- technology that is needed but not available
- services needed that are associated with technology (what services patrons currently use, how often, and what options are available for other training)
- training considerations for technology (how patrons currently receive training and what options exist for other training)

**How will the information be collected?** Quantitative information can be collected with usage statistics, surveys, questionnaires, or polls. Qualitative information can be collected with focus groups, observations, and interviews. Specific examples will be provided below under "Types of Assessments."

**How will the results be analyzed and disseminated?** Creating the plan for the needs assessment and administering the assessment can be time intensive. However, the value really emerges with the analyses, decisions, and dissemination of results and plans. Make sure to also plan for the following:

- Who will do statistical analysis? Do you have the appropriate software and expertise for the analysis?
- Does evidence show that there is a gap in meeting the goals and mission of the library?
- Who will prepare the results and rank-ordered list of recommendations?
- How will you communicate your findings?

Part of the needs assessment plan should be the time frame for conducting the assessment components. For some institutions, this may be required as part of an institutional review board (IRB) process. The need to obtain approval from an institutional review board prior to administering any surveys or conducting focus groups or interviews can delay the start of the project for several months. At many institutions, all human-subject research projects must be reviewed and approved before human subjects can be recruited or involved in research activities. For public and school libraries, even if there is not an official IRB process, there may be some local requirements for getting permission to conduct research. In schools, parents of minors usually need to receive the research study, including protocols for assuring user privacy, confidentiality, and rights, and then sign a consent form.

## Types of Assessments

There are several effective ways to gather information about technology needs, including informal feedback as well as more formal approaches such as surveys, focus groups, interviews, and polls. This section describes these methods.

### Informal Feedback

You may already have some ideas about the type of equipment and services that are needed based on conversations with patrons who have asked for certain equipment or services. This may include previous tracking of the number of times patrons have asked for a piece of equipment or for training, workshops, or programming in using the equipment. Throughout the year, this type of feedback should be collected. However, periodically, a formal assessment can be used to gather specific, focused information.

### Surveys and Questionnaires

Common assessment practices are surveys and questionnaires. These can be either in print or on the web. Surveys and questionnaires measure areas such as student satisfaction with services, programs, and collections, and can be used to determine the library's future direction in those areas. Several methods can be used to survey users, including in-person polls as well as print and web surveys and questionnaires. Free software such as SurveyMonkey (https://www.surveymonkey.com/) is available for online surveys. Subscription options such as Qualtrics (http://qualtrics.com/) can also be used if funds are available or if the institution already has a subscription. The following surveys from the Minnesota Department of Education are good examples to follow when constructing your survey. The first two surveys were distributed to Minnesota teachers to ask about their use of technology in the classroom; this information can be used to assist in the technology planning process. The third survey was distributed more broadly and asks questions pertaining to educational-technology usage and needs.

Technology—Instructional Practices Survey: https://education.state.mn.us/mdesurvey/index.php?sid=16773&lang=en

Technology—Instructional Practices Survey (PDF of all questions): http://education.state.mn.us/mdeprod/idcplg?IdcService=GET_FILE&dDocName=001984&RevisionSelectionMethod=latestReleased&Rendition=primary

Educational Technology Needs Assessment: http://www.surveymonkey.com/s.aspx?sm=lSsWCYRNQ56LYjmZiaIuwA_3d_3d

## Survey Design Tips

When testing, consider the following in the design elements and collector settings.

1. Did you include a clear introduction explaining who you are, what the survey is about, how long it will take, and how to move through the survey?
2. If there are terms that need to be defined, have you defined them?
3. Did you include open-ended comment boxes for each question in case the respondents want to add something else?
4. In the case of web surveys, did you turn off the "required to answer" option for the survey? Respondents should be allowed to skip questions. If not, they may just quit the survey.
5. Did you allow participants to go back and edit a response?
6. If there is an incentive that was being advertised for taking the survey, such as entry into a drawing, did you include an option for participants to enter their name and e-mail information?
7. Is there a "Thank You" page thanking respondents for their time and providing follow-up contact information if they want to discuss the topic further?
8. Did you specify an end date when the survey closes?

Regardless of the platform for your web survey (an institutional option or a free web option), the questions and options should be reviewed for clarity, jargon, and accuracy. Ask several students, patrons, and staff members to take the survey as a pilot run to get their feedback for revisions. The pretest pilot of the survey provides two functions. First, it serves as the initial "live" test. Second, it is the last step in finalizing the survey questions and format. The pilot offers feedback on whether the survey's wording is clear to all respondents and whether the questions mean the same thing to all respondents. You can also verify how the collector settings work.

## Checklist for the Pilot

The following is a good checklist of concerns that you, as the survey designer, should consider during the pilot. This is adapted from Iraossi (2006, 90–92):

- Do the respondents understand the objective of the survey?
- Is the wording of the survey clear?
- Are the answer choices compatible with the respondents' experience in the matter?
- Do any of the items require the respondents to think too long or hard before responding? If so, which ones?
- Do any of the items produce irritation, embarrassment, or confusion?
- Do any of the questions generate response bias? If so, which ones?
- Do the answers collected reflect what you want in regard to the purpose of the survey?
- Is there enough variety in the answers received? If not, perhaps the question needs to be rephrased to elicit a broader range of responses.
- Is the survey too long?
- According to your test audience, have any other important issues been overlooked?

## Publicizing and Disseminating the Survey

Once you have revised the survey and again tested it, you can add it to your web pages and send it out to your potential audience with a preface about what the survey is and how the responses will help the library in implementing a loanable technology program, especially in determining the type of equipment and services to provide. Make sure you include a closing date for the survey and your contact information in case the participant has questions. You may want to consider offering incentives for taking the survey, such as the participant's name being put into a drawing for a tech item prize, for example. It can also be a good strategy to preface the announcement with something that will get the participant's attention, like this: "Would you like to borrow cameras, voice recorders, laptops, and other technology from the library? If so, please take this short ten-minute survey to let us know your preferences."

A good practice is to resend the notice a few days before the close of the survey, thanking those who already submitted the survey and mentioning that there are two days left for users to give feedback about the type of technology they would like to see the library offer for checkout.

## Additional Tips for Print Surveys

The print version of the web survey can also be made available in the library with a box next to it for people to deposit the survey. A colorful marker board with images of loanable technology can serve as an attention getter to direct people to the survey. Figure 2.1 illustrates an example of a marker board calling attention to a survey. An advantage of the in-house print version of the survey is that it will gather feedback from active users of the library who may have experience with what the library does or does not offer. An example of a survey used in this instance is included in appendix B.

## Poll Questions and Point-of-Contact Surveys

Another way to gather feedback from users in the library is to hand out brief polls when patrons check out materials, or place the polls on a marker board, as described above. Staff at the University of Illinois at Urbana-Champaign periodically use this method. They keep the box at the circulation desk and mention that if users return the poll, they

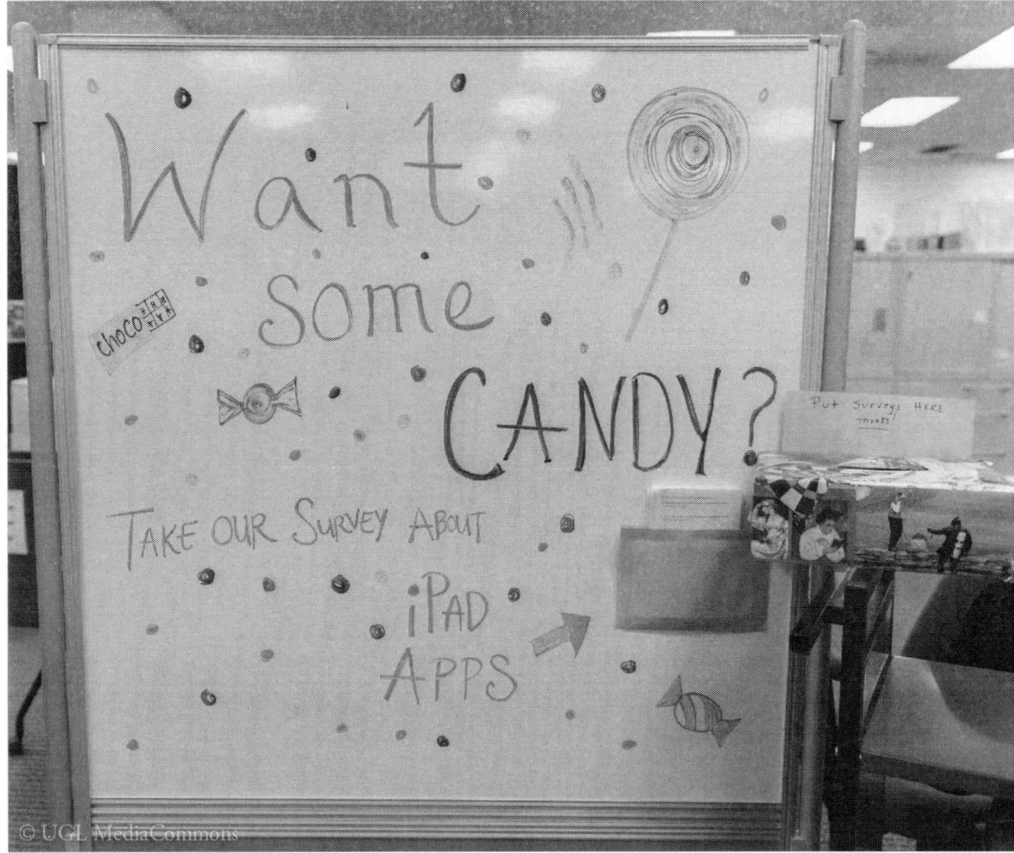


**Figure 2.1.** Image of Marker Board Questions

can take a piece of candy. These quick polls take only a minute of someone's time but can provide valuable feedback.

## Focus Group Sessions

Effective focus groups typically consist of eight to ten participants, which can include students, faculty, staff, and community members. The facilitator uses broad questions that are scripted and prevetted to make sure they are not leading. It is best to use a facilitator not involved with the project to ensure impartiality. One person can facilitate while another records the responses. A useful technique is to project the notes on a large screen so participants can see the points, revisit them, and add other comments.

Results from questionnaires are often used as topics to be explored further in focus-group interviews. Students, patrons, and faculty can be invited to participate in a series of focus groups pertaining to specific questions. Responses can be valuable in helping to learn about particular uses for types of equipment and additional aspects to include in a program. The results of this evaluation can expand the researchers' knowledge of the participants' experience with loanable technology and editing services, as well as the participants' views on needs for particular technology, services, training, and access. This feedback can also lay the groundwork to improve and develop the learning environment and other related library services.

One suggestion for focus groups is to provide pizza and beverages as an incentive to participate. It is also useful to have individuals sign up for a particular time slot (with their contact information) so a reminder can be sent. In some environments, it may also be possible to have impromptu focus groups, for whomever is in the library, by making an announcement such as: "Right now the library is looking for ten individuals to spend thirty minutes with us to give us feedback on our loanable technology program. Free pizza for the first ten individuals who come to room 295." If more people come than you can accommodate, ask if those who responded would like to come to the next section (and give that time and date).

Focus groups can be extremely valuable because one participant's comments remind another participant of an experience or example and a great conversation ensues. The responses can help library services and spaces continuously evolve. Following are some suggestions for conducting a focus group:

- Once participants are gathered in the room, introduce yourselves and give a brief explanation of the purpose of this session.
- Ask the participants to brainstorm in response to a question (see textbox 2.4 for sample questions) while you record the responses on a board or in an Excel document that you can project for all to see (this is where having an assistant to record the responses comes in handy).
- Leave time so that you can direct the participants to look back at the list and reflect on which of these services and technologies they would actually visit or use at the library.
- Try to have the participants look at the overall list and rank each item according to priority of importance (important, somewhat important, or not very important).
- At the end of the session, give participants an involvement card if they would like to participate in the future conversations. This card should have your contact information and topic of interest (e.g., Loanable Technology Feedback).

### TEXTBOX 2.4

### SAMPLE FOCUS-GROUP QUESTIONS FOR LOANABLE TECHNOLOGY PROGRAMS

- What types of technologies do you now use for your classes, projects, and activities?
- Do any of your classes or job duties require you to prepare reports or projects using multimedia? Follow up with questions to determine which classes or duties, what types of projects, what technologies they require, and where the participants get these technologies.
- What technologies would you want provided in this library?
- What technologies would you want to be able to check out from the library?
- How do you learn to use the equipment, software, hardware, and peripherals that you use? Follow up with questions to determine the specifics (i.e., people, places, online sources).
- What do you expect this library to offer in terms of technology training or support?

### Interviews

Interviews are excellent opportunities to talk in depth with individuals to learn about their experiences and suggestions on a particular topic. For loanable technology, interviews with stakeholders, such as faculty, information technology specialists, and administrators, could provide specific examples of expectations for multimedia in both classes and the library. Specific recommendations and types of multimedia can be elicited, as well as information about other departments and programs also engaged in providing multimedia equipment and services. It would be preferable to tape the interviews, but again check if you are required to present IRB documentation.

## Analyzing the Data

As mentioned earlier, it is important to plan who will analyze the data, what software you have for this purpose, and what format you will use for reporting the information. The analysis should document statistics and patterns, identify gaps in a program, and offer suggestions. Think about what you want to do with this information and with whom you will be sharing the information. This will make a difference in how you present the data (tables, charts, infographics, word clouds). Once you have baseline data, you can use that data each year to show trends and patterns. The process of analyzing data is well beyond the scope of this book, but a good resource for helping with collecting and analyzing data is the Community Tool Box from the Work Group for Community Health and Development at the University of Kansas (http://ctb.ku.edu/en/table-of-contents/evaluate/evaluate-community-interventions/collect-analyze-data/main). This site discusses both quantitative and qualitative data.

## Ongoing Assessment

Even after a program has been established, you want to make sure you are assessing use, impact, and further need. Examples of this type of assessment include looking at:

- Usage stats: checkouts, classes supported, and types of equipment that circulate.
- Circulation of items: For example, provide regular comparisons of trends in usage of items to highlight any increases in use of particular items. This may indicate a need to purchase additional items of that type as well as potential training needs.
- Purpose for use: Document purpose each time an item is checked out, such as name of class or type of project. At the Undergraduate Library at the University of Illinois, when loanable technology items are checked out, the patron is asked if the item is for a class, and if so, which one. The patron is also asked if there is additional technology that he or she would like to see the library offer. Based on feedback, the library increased its offerings from thirty-six unique items (with multiple copies) to over 160 between 2010 and 2013. Most of the recent purchases have been higher-end cameras and equipment. Figure 2.2 provides a snapshot of a designated part of a loanable technology form that asks for suggestions for new technology.
- Unmet requests: Document when a request cannot be met and include date, item, and purpose. This can help in future planning if, for example, you note a particular

UNIVERSITY OF ILLINOIS AT URBANA – CHAMPAIGN: UNDERGRADUATE LIBRARY

**EQUIPMENT LOAN AGREEMENT**

Please indicate if this is being used for a class project: ___ Yes ___ No. If so, which class: ______________

**Figure 2.2.** Class-Use Questions on Loanable Technology Form

week when there are many requests for voice recorders or cameras. Is there a class project that is scheduled routinely at that time of the year? A conversation with the teacher or faculty member might help with preplanning to reserve items or to acquire additional items. Are there consistent requests from community members for an item? Is the request consistent throughout the year or only at certain times of the year? Tracking unmet requests can help determine additional purchases. Table 2.1 provides an example of a simple chart that can be used for this purpose.

Understanding the needs of the community you are serving with loanable technology is a first step in planning items to purchase, budget needs, and service implications for providing the equipment (training, staffing, support, processing). Libraries may also need to consider the standards and guidelines that they must follow related to technology.

When conducting a needs assessment or creating a technology plan, think about how the outcomes of the plan's implementation will be measured and evaluated. Benchmarks of existing services must be determined, direct and indirect measures must be identified, and a process to compare and evaluate the resultant measures to existing benchmarks and expectations must be designed. Dates for the release of progress reports should be included in the implementation plan.

Stakeholders need to be consulted and updated throughout the process as the loanable technology plan is developed. Communications to and from the planning committee and the stakeholders will keep everyone current, informed, and involved with the process. In addition, opportunities will present themselves during the bidirectional communications that will allow the planning committee to educate and inform the stakeholders about the library, its service roles, its future, and other critical matters. Do not miss these opportunities to explain and advocate the library's vision.

Developing a collaborative, well thought-out plan for the implementation and growth of your loanable technology program is important so that the time, expenses, and planning will support the mission, goals, and user needs. Through this process, an initial collection development policy for loanable technology can be drafted, yet it may take a few years to truly understand what the library can (or realistically should) support and what the focus will be for items to collect.

**Table 2.1.** Tracking Requests

| ITEM | DATE | PURPOSE (CLASS/PROJECT) | FACULTY/ STUDENT/STAFF | OTHER |
|---|---|---|---|---|
| | | | | |
| | | | | |
| | | | | |

## Key Points

When planning for a needs assessment for your library's loanable technology plan, keep in mind the following key points:

- It is useful to create a technology plan that details existing resources, equipment, and services as well as short- and long-term goals for the future.
- Creating the plan for the needs assessment and administering the assessment will take considerable effort. However, the value really emerges with the analyses, decisions, and dissemination of results and plans.
- Even after a program has been established, you want to make sure you are assessing use, impact, and further need on an ongoing basis.

The next chapter will discuss the development of a loanable technology collection as well as considerations for purchasing and maintaining the collection.

## References


Cohn, John M., and Ann L. Kelsey. 2009. *The Complete Library Technology Planner: A Guidebook with Sample Technology Plans and RFPs.* New York: Neal-Schuman Publishers.

Dugan, Robert E. 2002. "Information Technology Plans." *Journal of Academic Librarianship* 28, no. 3 (May): 152–56.

Iraossi, Giuseppe. 2006. *The Power of Survey Design: A User's Guide for Managing Surveys, Interpreting Results, and Influencing Respondents.* Washington, D.C.: World Bank Publications.

CHAPTER 3

# Determining Types of Equipment to Purchase

**IN THIS CHAPTER**

- ▷ Creating an effective advisory group for the selection of loanable technology equipment to purchase
- ▷ Steps for the planning process
- ▷ Strategies to determine the most effective types of equipment to purchase for patron use, including benefits, challenges, concerns, and suggestions when contemplating purchasing and circulating these items
- ▷ Suggestions for high-end equipment if you want to move beyond the basic technologies

EQUIPMENT SELECTION AND purchase is the pivotal step in the creation of a loanable technology program and requires the greatest amount of budget and resources. It does not need to carry with it a large deal of stress; rather, with a little strategic planning it can be an easy step that then builds into an efficient and user-friendly loanable technology program. Facets of the planning include: developing a loanable technology collection development policy, understanding the budget that is available, and establishing an advisory group to help make decisions on both the direction of the program and the purchases. Chapter 4 will discuss budget in more detail, and chapter 7 will provide an overview for policies, including collection development. This chapter will provide some suggestions and examples for creating an advisory group that can help decide which equipment to offer for a program, as well as parameters for a program, both initially and in subsequent stages. The chapter also highlights various options for equipment purchases.

## Advisory Group

The selection of hardware and equipment can have the heaviest effect on the overall budget of your loanable technology program. A tempting approach for many might be to order every popular bleeding-edge technology that has recently been released, as it will be flashy and popular among patrons wishing to have access, but that can result in a quickly blown budget. Also, new equipment does not have the in-depth technical support and robust Internet community that can assist in providing easy solutions when problems arise. With this in mind, it is important to spend an appropriate amount of time in the planning and selection of this equipment and to involve others who have experience or knowledge in technology use and acquisition, as well as members of the community who will be using the equipment.

### Who Should Be Involved?

The lead person for the group may be the library's department head, director, media specialist, information technology expert, or loanable technology program coordinator. For best representation, make sure the advisory group includes experts in technology, purchasing and acquisitions, budget, facilities, and management. This group can offer varying guidance that will result in a more thought-out consensus on the merits of each technology category. Several factors may influence who should be involved with the advisory group, such as the size of the school, the departments you have enlisted to assist, technology groups that might have knowledge of the technology purchased, and the extent of the budget. Someone from the library's information technology (IT) group should be part of the group to advise on how well the equipment will interface with library computers or public equipment. Additionally, for public libraries, there should be representation from the library trustees and at least two community members who have demonstrated interest in loanable technology. Because of the intersection between public and school libraries, it would also be helpful to include a media specialist or librarian from the school system who can detail how students are using technology and what they might seek from the public library. These individuals can offer perspectives from the board and the community. In addition to including someone from the budget group and IT, advisory groups for schools will probably need an administrator, a couple of teachers who have an active focus toward utilizing multimodal projects in their curriculum, and a couple of students who are knowledgeable about media editing and the equipment that would help others in creating technology projects.

The individual in charge of initiating the library loanable technology program should take the role of coordinator and make contact with the people chosen for the initial equipment-purchase planning meetings. As part of this role, the coordinator should send out an agenda prior to the meetings, make sure that minutes are taken, determine who will be responsible for accomplishing action items, set deadlines, and follow up with the individuals. Textbox 3.1 gives an example of an agenda that illustrates some key points to be discussed at a first meeting.

Recognize that the participants are also busy, so make sure to send out any documents, reports, draft statements, and suggested lists of technology to purchase ahead of time. In the e-mail reminder before the meeting, reiterate what you hope to accomplish at the meeting, such as: refine the draft mission statement; discuss the scope of the program; list the first-tier and second-tier technology to purchase, along with how many of

**TEXTBOX 3.1**

**EXAMPLE OF AN AGENDA**

1. Introductions of members and their role with technology
2. Mission and scope of loanable technology program
3. Brainstorming of possible categories of technology to offer
   a. Suggestions based on needs assessment
   b. Other
4. Considerations for equipment to be chosen
   a. Ease of use
   b. Cost
   c. Support
5. Possible online retailers for the purchase of equipment
6. Action items and next steps

each category of equipment are necessary. Be careful not to get bogged down in hardware specifics. In terms of technology, you could easily spend the majority of the meeting discussing the merits of buying a tablet with twice as much RAM versus the base model. These types of conversations can occur individually (outside the meeting) or as e-mails. Use your group to discuss higher-level questions: "Do we want to provide tablets at all?" or "What general features in a tablet might best serve our patrons?" The model number and other more granular choices will come later and do not need to involve a committee.

## Discussions for Setting Parameters for the Loanable Technology Program

Prior to selecting the equipment, it will be important to establish the specific goals to be accomplished with the program. Some of this was discussed in chapter 2, and the results of the needs assessment should help guide the conversation about the focus of the program. It may also be that the needs assessment does not occur until after the advisory group meets. Often it is an advisory group that plans for a needs assessment. The following are questions that the advisory group should discuss to help frame the types of loanable technology purchases:

- What do you want the main focus or goal of your loanable tech program to be?
- What is the desired size and scope of the loanable tech program?
- Are there funds for both initial and recurring purchases?

**1. What do you want the main focus or goal of your loanable tech program to be?** The following are questions that should be discussed at the beginning in order to have a shared understanding of the intent of the program. The response to each question will help guide decisions to be made.

- Is the goal of the loanable technology program to provide research and study tools in order to assist patrons?
- Is a priority of the program to provide equipment in a specific area such as audio/video or digital media?

- Is it important to provide patrons with access to cutting-edge technology or is it more important to provide tested and stable versions of a type of technology?

**2. What is the desired size and scope of the loanable technology program?** To answer this question, it will be important to know the budget. A fuller discussion of the budget will be provided in chapter 4. Budget will usually be a limiting factor when considering the types of loanable technology to purchase. After determining the focus and goals of the desired program, compare that to the proposed budget. This comparison will help formulate an idea of the size and scope of the program to be created. It may be that you will need to modify original goals in purchases by creating stages for purchasing items or by choosing a model that may be a step down from the highest end in order to reduce costs or to provide more items of a specific type to patrons. As an example of cost savings, see table 3.1 for a cost comparison of various 2013 iPad Air models (using prices available at the Apple retail store at the time of writing).

**Table 3.1.** Cost Comparison of 2013 iPad Air Models

| PRODUCT | COST |
|---|---|
| 2013 iPad Air 32 GB | $599 |
| 2013 iPad Air 16 GB | $499 |
| 2013 iPad Air Mini Retina | $399 |

The advisory group will need to decide if it is more important to go with the newest model but purchase fewer iPads or go with the previous model and provide more iPads. As an example, table 3.2 gives a breakdown of what you could buy if your library had determined a budget of $5,000 to spend on iPads.

**Table 3.2.** Comparison of Project Purchase for $5,000 Budget

| PRODUCT | COST | TABLETS PURCHASED WITH A $5,000 BUDGET |
|---|---|---|
| 2013 iPad Air 32 GB | $599 | 8 |
| 2013 iPad Air 16 GB | $499 | 10 |
| 2013 iPad Mini Retina | $399 | 12 |

When assessing whether or not to go with an earlier model, the group will need to make sure to discuss features that must be included (such as sufficient memory to store and run apps). The members of the group can contribute their perspectives on what they understand the needs of the patrons to be with a particular piece of equipment. They will need to review results from the needs assessment and further discuss choices with some of the patrons. That is why it is useful to include members from the user community on the advisory committee. With their input, it may be clearer if an earlier model will provide the needed features (or space capacity), thus stretching the budget to allow for purchasing more items.

**3. Are there funds for both initial and recurring purchases?** Most technology equipment has a shelf life of two to four years, depending on the quality of the product and the frequency of patron use. Any loanable technology program without recurring funds will probably see its usage drop as the age of the product increases and its overall functionality decreases. Budgeting and funding options will be discussed in chapter 4; however, be advised that funds for replacement of loanable technology should be included in the budget for a loanable technology program.

## Equipment for In-Library or Out-of-Library Checkout

Once the advisory group has decided on the type and quantity of technology to purchase (given the budget) you can begin researching specific products, including which ones might be available for in-library use only or available for checkout. The group will need to determine how many days (or weeks) to allow for a checkout period. This will need to be a local determination and may be based on how much equipment is available. Will it be for three days, one week, two weeks, or some other option? Will the equipment be allowed to be reserved ahead of time or renewed? Chapter 8 will provide more guidance on checking out and reserving materials.

### In-Library Use Only Technology

The "in-library use" technology is for patron use within the library and would allow use for a specified time period, such as for one or two hours, in order to maximize availability among the greatest amount of patrons. The equipment that you will want to offer for in-library use only will be those items that are repeatedly asked for by patrons to use in the library or equipment that was identified through assessments.

The first category of items that might be purchased and available for in-library use are calculators, graphing calculators, chargers, USB drives, power cords, game controllers or devices, or anything that will help a patron do homework or use their own devices while in the library.

A second common category of equipment for in-library use is laptops and tablets. Laptops available for in-library use can augment the public terminals that are available. If the needs assessment determined that patrons typically access web resources while on computers in the library, then laptops (or tablets) could be excellent resources for them to use while in the library (especially if there are limited numbers of permanent computers available in the library). Your advisory group may also decide to offer some of these to be checked out of the library. In that case, you may want to clearly designate a certain number to purchase for in-library use and some that can be used out of the library. In either case, the advisory committee will want to decide on a maximum number of any item to purchase for the first year and subsequent years, with some decision being made as to the total number of graphing calculators, voice recorders, cameras, or laptops, for example, to have in the collection. The goal for in-library-use items is to accommodate as many students as possible for short-term use of equipment.

### Out-of-Library-Use Checkout Technology

The other category of equipment, which may encompass the majority of the loanable technology inventory, is the "out-of-library use" technology. Examples of equipment that many libraries allow to circulate (although the categories below are very general) include:

- adapters, cables, and miscellaneous items (headphones, calculators, GPS devices, VCR/DVD players, voice editors)
- cameras and equipment (microphones, voice recorders, tripods, video and audio accessories, portable lights, projectors, webcams)
- games and accessories (game controllers, portable gaming consoles)
- memory and external drives (USB flash drives, external hard drives, memory cards, memory-card readers, DVD drives and writers)
- mobile and portable devices (DVD players, tablets, MP3 players, radio/cassette players)

Each library will need to decide who is able to check out these items and with which type of identification. It may be a valid library card, a form signed by a parent or teacher, or a community card. Each library will need to establish the length of checkout time (as mentioned above).

Some of the most popular types of technologies that libraries provide for patron use are e-book readers, tablet computers, cameras, and accessories. The next sections discuss some benefits, challenges, concerns, and suggestions related to purchasing and circulating these items.

## E-book Readers

E-book (electronic book) readers are portable digital devices that act as a reader and storage device for digital books, newspapers, magazines, and other traditional print media. Many other types of portable digital devices, such as smartphones and tablets, can also display various formats of electronic books; however, e-book readers are devices that are more or less solely devoted to this one function. They tend to maximize battery life and display quality. Many use a technology called e-ink (electronic ink), which more accurately imitates the feel of reading a traditional book or newspaper and uses a fraction of the energy of other tablet and smartphone display technology.

Libraries have a variety of ways that they provide these e-readers, as well as their content. Some libraries load programs and books on the e-readers and check them out. Others have a subscription to a content package (such as OverDrive) that allows patrons to download e-books that may be connected to a particular service (such as Amazon or Barnes and Noble). Axis 360 is a product that is not platform dependent and is also ADA compliant. Digital licensing for electronic books can be tricky, and each library will need to check licensing and local requirements. The University of Illinois at Urbana-Champaign (UIUC) loans out various types of e-readers and iPads and leaves it to the patron to acquire their own content based on source or personal retailer preference.

E-readers can be low-cost items, have a longer shelf life than laptops, require lower power, and have a long battery life (potentially up to one month). However, some of the challenges include negotiating licensing agreements for that product and, if you subscribe to the e-reader content package, figuring out whether the content on the reader is ADA compliant. These are issues that that each library will need to take into account. It is also possible now to download the apps for e-readers to phones and tablets, thus providing options on those devices for reading e-book content designated for a particular brand. For example, a Kindle app exists for most major mobile devices, giving users a little more freedom outside of specific Kindle devices to read e-books purchased through Amazon.

## TEXTBOX 3.2

### POPULAR BRANDS AND MODELS OF E-READERS

- Amazon Kindle, including Traditional Kindle, Kindle Paperwhite, and Kindle Fire: http://www.amazon.com/dp/B00I15SB16/ref=kods_xs_dp_oos
- Barnes and Noble Nook, including Nooks and tablets: http://www.barnesandnoble.com/u/Compare-NOOKs/379003181
- Kobo Aura: http://www.kobo.com/devices#ereaders
- Ectaco jetBook: http://www.jetbook.net
- Ematic eGlide Reader: http://www.ematic.us/readers/egl101

These options are helpful to explore, especially for libraries that subscribe to packages such as OverDrive or My Media Mall, in order to provide flexibility and options for patrons who want to download e-content from the library. Libraries will need to determine if there are devices that are optimal for e-reader packages they purchase or whether packages require a specific device or vendor. Explore the reviews and comparisons that are offered and contact other libraries that use e-readers to hear firsthand of their experiences.

## Tablet Computers (Tablets)

A tablet computer, or tablet, is a general-purpose device that contains all the common parts of a computer in a single panel. Tablets are most often controlled via touch or gesture. Patrons predominantly use tablet computers as media-consumption devices to check websites, social media, videos, or e-mail. However, mobile devices increasingly are becoming a viable option for quality digital video and digital audio recordings, and they have capable apps for not only recording but also editing digital media. They are becoming very popular in instruction classes and workshops.

### Common Features of a Tablet

The following features are standard in tablets but may differ in specific capacities, so it is important to review these for each product.

- camera (video and still)
- microphone
- high-definition digital touchscreen
- digital storage
- rechargeable battery

Until recently, Apple's iPad was the most popular tablet, and many libraries have experimented in using them for instruction and reference, as well as for circulation. There are now many alternative tablet options with similar features available to libraries, and they are often cheaper than iPads. A later section details the experience at UIUC using iPads and notes important points to be aware of when working with the Apple platform.

## TEXTBOX 3.3

### POPULAR TABLET BRANDS

- Apple iPad: http://www.apple.com/ipad
- Google Nexus: http://www.google.com/nexus/tablets/
- Samsung Galaxy Tab: http://www.samsung.com/us/mobile/galaxy-tab
- Microsoft Surface: http://www.microsoft.com/surface/en-us
- Amazon Kindle Fire: http://www.amazon.com/dp/B00HCNHDN0/ref=fs_fs
- Lenovo tablets: http://shop.lenovo.com/us/en/tablets/

## Apple iPad and the Apple Platform

The Apple iPad has been marketed as a high-end digital device with an intuitive interface that is easy to learn and possesses a high visual aesthetic. The first iPad was released in 2010, with the current version, the iPad Air 2, being the equivalent of the sixth generation of iPad. UIUC purchased iPads for several purposes. Reference librarians use them to be able to rove around the library rather than being tied to a desk. Student assistants use an iPad mini at a satellite desk, which allows them to look something up for a patron while shelving materials or staffing the checkpoint downstairs. The iPad is also used in kiosk stations to display the following: support pages pertaining to the media commons, projects created using loanable technology, and media-editing resources at the library; loanable technology resources; and mobile apps created to help users navigate the library. Figure 3.1 shows the use of iPads at reference and student stations.

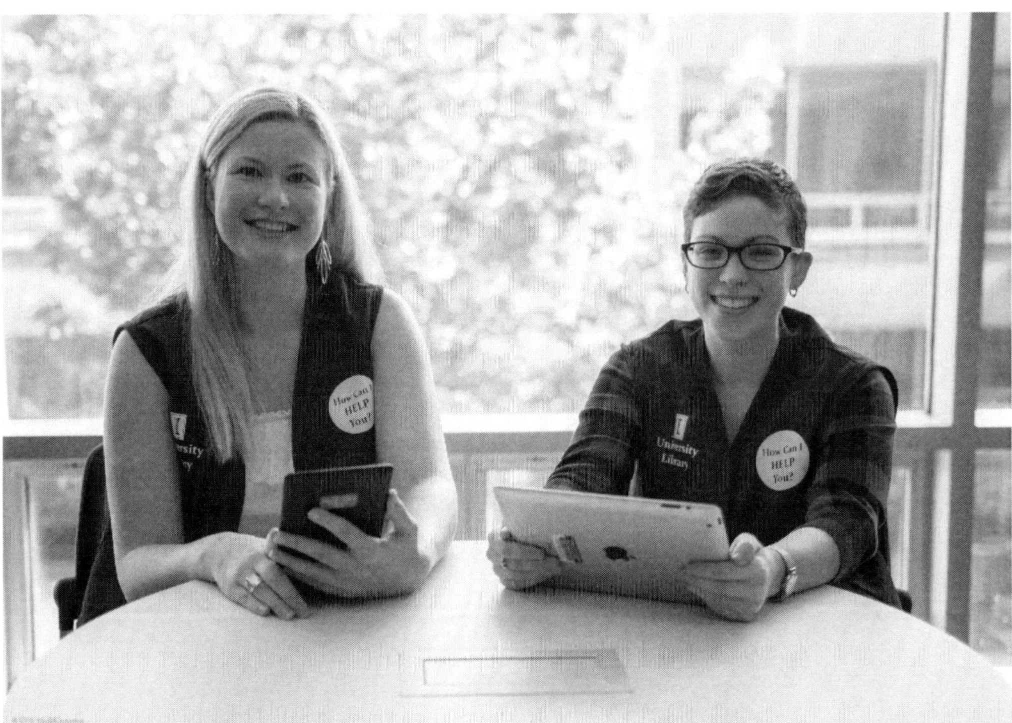


**Figure 3.1.** Images of iPad Use at the Reference and Student Café Tables

At UIUC twenty iPads were purchased as out-of-library circulating items to explore whether they could supplement or replace the use of laptops. However, this plan resulted in some challenges. While Apple has never specifically stated this, the idea behind Apple's iOS-based products is that they will have one owner—if not for the life of the device, then certainly for a longer term. This is a reasonable expectation, given that the majority of consumers purchase an Apple iOS device as a personal device, but it does pose a small problem in a loanable technology environment. An example of this is that iOS devices do not currently have the ability to do multiuser logins. Presently, a user wishing to take advantage of the majority of the functions of an iOS device would need to log in or create an Apple ID, which would then tie them to the device. This log-in is fairly pervasive in that the user needs to use the log-in only once and the device will apply it automatically for any other function requiring an Apple ID. This concept will be further explained, and possible solutions offered, later in this chapter.

## Functions That Require an Apple ID

Following are some of the common functions that require an Apple ID. It is important to understand the functions listed and their benefits, as they may not be available to users depending on how the iPads are configured to operate. This can be frustrating to users, as the functionalities listed below, when taken as a whole, are a fairly considerable portion of why patrons are interested in iPads. This is why the pros and cons of an Apple ID should be clearly understood when planning the configuration strategy of user-loanable iOS devices.

**iTunes.** Apple's online store to purchase digital music, videos, and television shows. A credit card is required to be tied to the Apple ID before purchases in iTunes can be made.

**iBooks and Newsstand.** Apps from Apple (free downloads) that are used for books and magazines, respectively.

**App Store.** While technically this falls under iTunes, iOS has a separate app specifically to find and download iOS apps. Mobile applications (apps) are small software applications designed for mobile devices. Whereas apps used to have specific versions for iPhone and iPad platforms, most popular applications are currently available to work on both iPhones and iPads. Apps form the majority of what makes a digital tablet a powerful and versatile device. Apps in the App Store can be either free or paid apps. Paid apps require credit card information that is tied to the Apple ID.

**iCloud.** iCloud is a Cloud-based backup and synchronization service. In this case "Cloud" is lingo for a secure network-accessible storage space for user data. For Apple iOS devices this currently serves two main purposes. First, it allows you to back up a variety of iOS user data, including:

- Contacts
- Calendars
- Documents and data
- Find My iPad
- Keychain (log-ins, passwords, credit card information, etc.)
- Mail
- Notes
- Photos
- Reminders

- Safari (Internet bookmarks)
- Storage and backup (app data)

Second, iCloud allows you to synchronize your applications and user data between multiple devices. For example, if a user owned an iPhone and an iPad, they would have the ability to make changes on one device and see those changes reflected on the other device simultaneously. This of course varies based on specific settings, applications, and network data access.

**Find my iPad.** An Apple-specific application that allows you to locate your iOS device. It offers useful options, such as the ability to remotely wipe (erase all content), play an audible noise (even if on mute), or turn off the device. This app can come in handy when attempting to locate a lost or stolen iOS device.

## Multiple Users for iPads?

Given all the functionality that requires an Apple ID and the idea that the Apple ID is then tied specifically to the device, it is very difficult to configure an iPad for multiple users or to distribute it in loanable technology with a generic Apple ID. Paid applications and purchases within iTunes require credit card information tied to an Apple ID. This eliminates the possibility of a generic Apple ID or multiple anonymous patrons using the same Apple ID. Note that if the Apple ID portion is skipped during configuration, the iPad will remind and ask the user to create an Apple ID anytime they wish to use a function that would require an Apple ID.

## Passcode and iOS Security

As a point of security, iOS devices offer the option of enabling a passcode. See figure 3.2 for an example of this. Per Apple support documentation, the passcode will be required when the following events occur:

- turn on or restart the device
- wake the device or unlock the screen (you can specify the amount of time the screen must be locked before requiring a passcode: http://support.apple.com/kb/ht4113)

Additional security is offered beginning with the iPhone 5s in the form of a biometric scanner. The biometric scanner records an image of the user's thumbprint and then uses that image as a way to identify the user in the future. This will probably begin showing up in other iOS devices as they are released. Again, this feature will make it difficult to loan out equipment if the device recognizes only one thumbprint.

## Privacy

User data privacy is certainly an issue when considering all of the information that can potentially be entered while using an iOS device. An iPad can hold user log-in and password data, credit card information, and user-specific data like address and other demographic material. More importantly, it holds the data of third-party apps that the user is

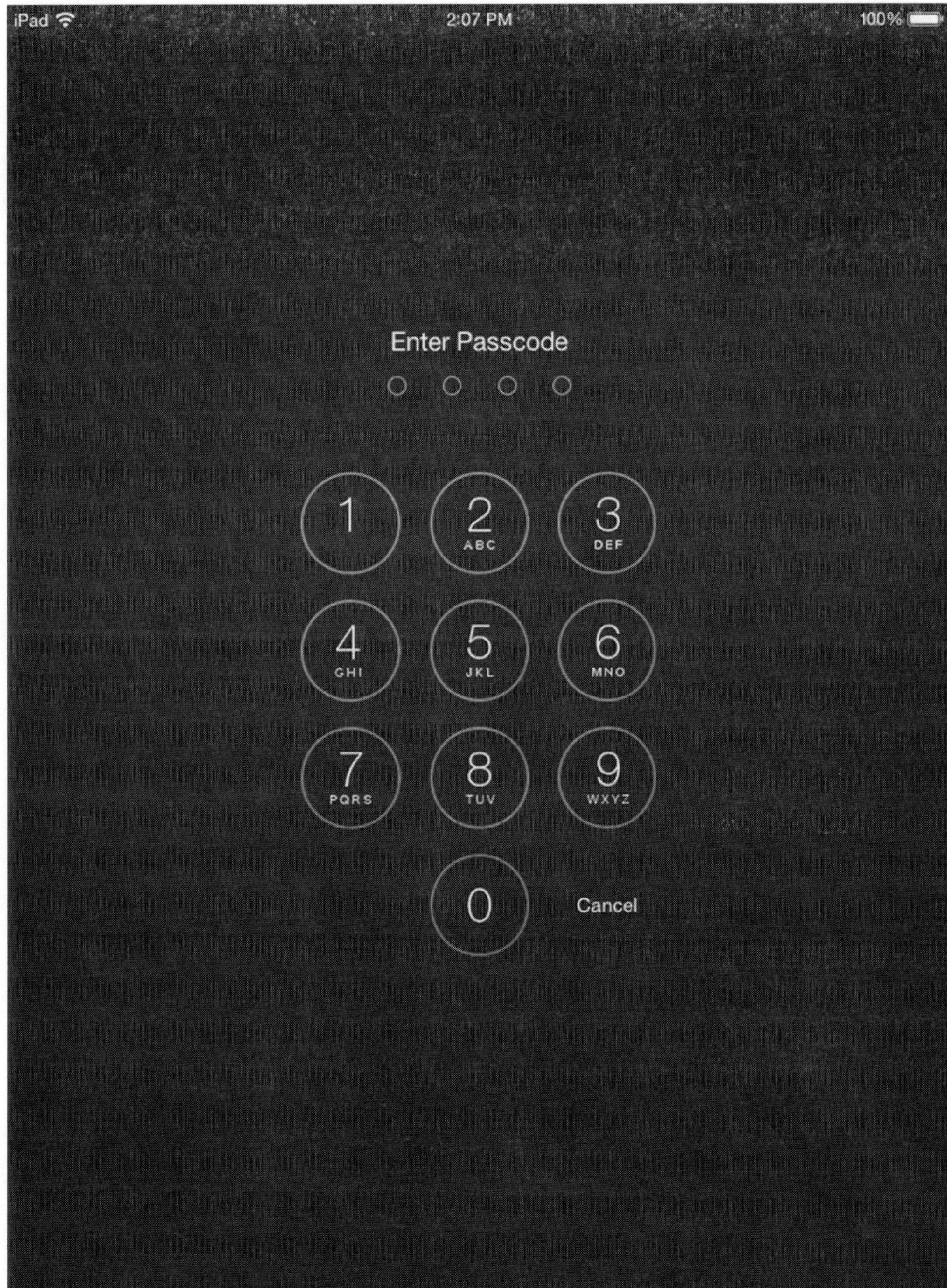


**Figure 3.2.** Screenshot of Passcode and iOS Security

logged into, and most of these applications have a persistent log-in, meaning that a user enters the log-in and password once and the app remains logged in for varying amounts of time (based on the app). Depending on the app, user information that might be on the device could include social-media information, bank records and access, financial history and information, and health records. Because of the sheer number of iOS apps available on a widely varying range of topics, there is almost an infinite amount of data that is potentially on an iPad that a user may not have wiped before it is returned to the library.

The privacy concern is one of the primary factors when establishing how to deploy and configure the iOS devices that will be used. With this in mind, iOS devices have several options for erasing user data, which will be discussed below.

## Configuration of iPads

Tablets and iPads can be preconfigured in a secure manner for patron use. This saves a lot of time and resources in having to individually set up each iPad and then having to reconfigure it every time it is returned. This process is called "configuration." A library currently has two options for the configuration and deployment of iPads and other iOS devices: unmanaged or managed. They can be left completely unmanaged, meaning no settings are changed and no other information is entered. This leaves the devices completely open and unsecure. The other option is to configure them, which secures the devices or limits the access the patron has to the devices themselves. These are further described below.

**Unmanaged.** This option is to leave the device entirely unlocked. Once users check out the device, they enter their account information and do any app download or purchasing for themselves. Upon return of the device, the loanable technology department wipes the device back to default in order to clear out any private data and information.

**Managed.** The second option is to "manage" the device, which means securing the device such that users cannot modify the settings or install their own apps. The devices have preinstalled apps and settings that are of most value to the users of the loanable technology. The potential downsides of this approach are that it limits options for the users and that any purchased apps would be an incurred cost to the library and not the user. The main benefit of this option is that it provides greater security and consistency due to preestablished settings.

The factors above detail some of the struggles and benefits of choosing Apple iPads. Currently, tablet devices seem to be a preferred option for many loanable technology programs and one that can carry a heavy cost. It is important to understand the pros and cons of these devices and their ecosystem before embarking on a large financial investment.

## Android Platform

In addition to the popular iPad tablets and Apple products, there are many products available that use the Android platform. The Android operating system, when compared to iOS, is a more open system allowing users more freedom to make changes. This can be a benefit or a burden, depending on the user base. Settings and features may also vary based on the hardware manufacturer, as manufacturers will often add or modify applications and settings. Below are options that are unique to Android tablets, as compared to Apple iPads.

### Options Unique to the Android Operating System

**Multiuser.** The stock (unaltered) version of Android allows for a device to have multiple user logins. This is extremely useful for a loanable technology program, as it allows for an administrative user to maintain full access, while also allowing for the creation of a generic user for the patron. Administrators also have the ability to create the generic user log-in and leave it blank until the user logs in for the first time, when the device will ask the user to create a user profile. See figure 3.3 for an illustration of the log-in screen.

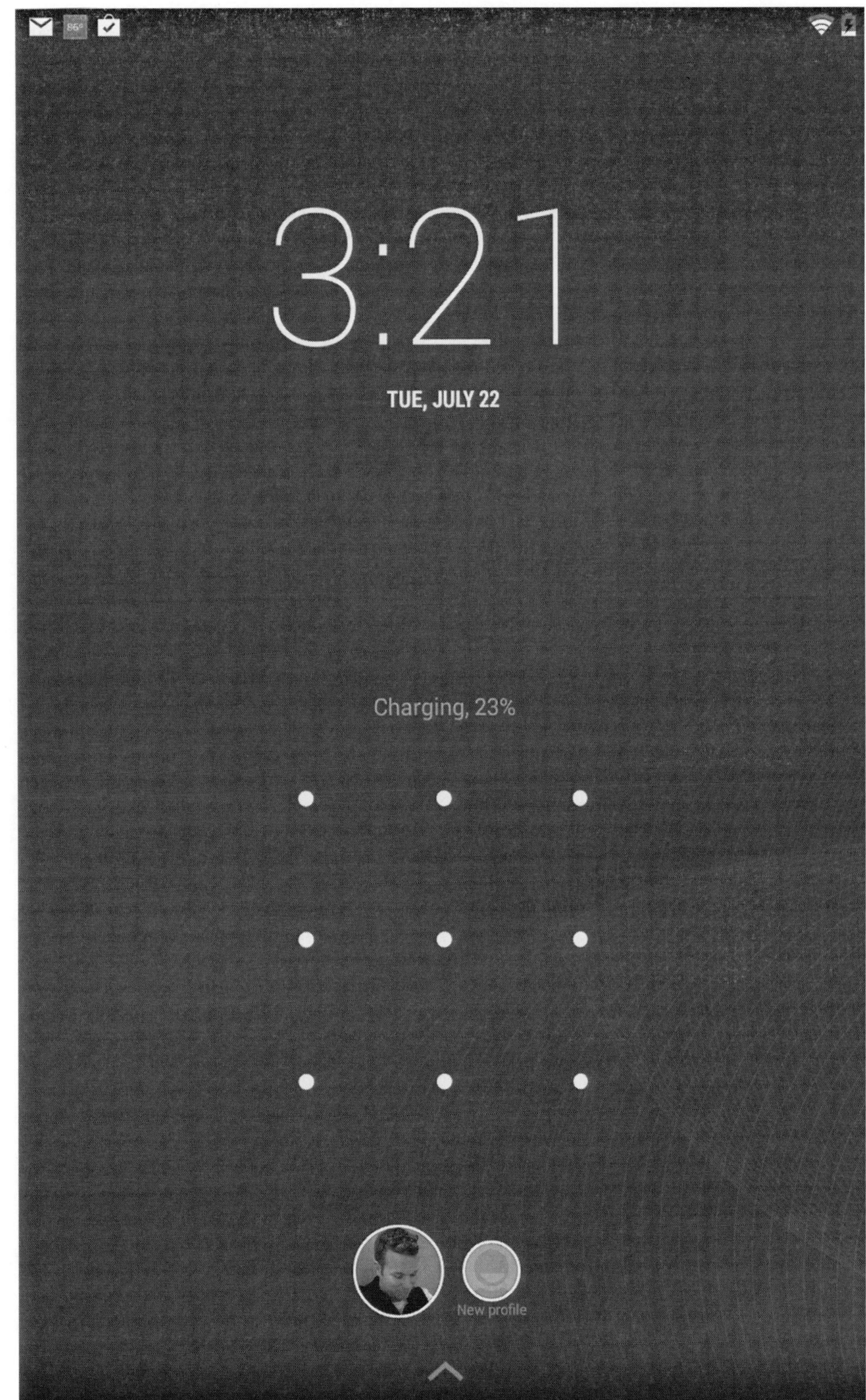


**Figure 3.3.** Multiple User Log-In Screenshot

**Boot to recovery.** One of the major concerns of adding tablets and other mobile devices to a loanable technology program is of a user hacking or modifying the device, making it difficult to reset it so it can be checked out to other users. If all goes wrong and the device is locked down or unusable, Android hardware allows for a "boot to recovery" option. This will erase everything from the device and restore to a default setup. While it can take a longer amount of time to process, it is extremely useful when all else fails.

**Charging cable.** Most Android hardware uses a standard micro-USB cable for charging and syncing. This eliminates the need to purchase a large variety of proprietary cables and third-party devices that may change or evolve with new versions of hardware. Figure 3.4 shows an image of this type of cable.

**Figure 3.4.** Image of Android Charging Cable

### Android versus iOS

As described in the section above, the Android platform has features that can make it potentially easier to support than the iOS iPads if tablets are to be used as a loanable technology item and if there will be a large number of patrons using them with short turnaround processing intervals. A downside of choosing Android over iOS is that iOS currently has a larger amount of developer support and offers a wider range of apps. While the Android platform may not be the final choice for a start-up loanable technology program, it has grown large enough and stable enough to at least be considered.

## Purchasing Mobile Applications

In addition to choosing the appropriate level and brand of tablet, your loanable technology program will also need to consider a variety of mobile applications. Most of the strengths and versatility found in a modern tablet device is in its ability to download or purchase third-party applications (apps). Apps are downloadable, self-contained software programs that add abilities beyond the applications provided on the mobile device by default. Applications come in two varieties: *paid*, which require credit card information or other suitable form of payment; and *free*, which can be downloaded with account information only. Libraries will need to decide if they want to establish an account that they can use to purchase apps to load to devices, or if they want to provide only the basic functions and let users access what they need from Internet-accessible storage (the Cloud).

## Media Equipment

With the increased demand and requirement of multimodal research projects, the need for digital video and audio equipment has grown, as has the support for helping patrons with their digital audio and video projects. One way to address the need for support is to develop a stronger focus on digital media equipment in a loanable technology program. Several categories of loanable technology that would support this effort are presented in the next section.

### Digital Still-Image Cameras

Also known as point-and-shoot cameras, these are user-friendly cameras that have a basic set of options but allow the user to turn the camera on and start shooting. Many of these cameras also have a "movie" function that allows for the recording of digital video. Figure 3.5 provides examples of still cameras. Resolution and size for images and video will be determined by the specific model purchased. Following are some of the features available in these cameras.

**Figure 3.5.** Images of Still Cameras

**Image size.** Cameras are often compared by the megapixel size of the image they take; the higher the megapixels, the larger the image. More importance should be placed on the quality of the image taken, which is obtained by a larger sensor. For example, many smartphones boast an image size of thirteen megapixels or larger but take that image on a very tiny sensor. If the lens and sensor are small, then the amount of light that can be let in is small and the camera can produce quality pictures only in very bright conditions. Look for a camera that takes quality images in low-light environments, which equates to most indoor scenarios.

**Video resolution.** As with image size, higher video resolutions are available in more expensive cameras. The current industry standard for professional-level video is 720p or 1080p, but video at that resolution will carry with it an added expense.

**TEXTBOX 3.4**

Video resolution is the number of lines of resolution on the screen at any moment in time. 1080p has 1080 lines of resolution on the screen. The full resolution would read as 1920*1080 for a widescreen image.

The intended use of the camera will determine if high-definition resolutions and the associated expenses are required. For example, video that will end up on the web or other smaller screens can have a lower resolution. Even an image resolution of 720p (much less than 1080p) is still considered high definition and is almost double the quality of a standard DVD (480p).

**Battery type.** Point-and-shoot cameras will either require a standard battery (AA or AAA) or provide a rechargeable battery of their own (usually lithium-ion). If the camera requires a standard AA battery, will your loanable technology program provide the batteries or ask the patron to do so? A provided rechargeable battery will require charging by staff or patrons but is reusable and more efficient.

## Video Cameras

Digital video cameras exist in a wide range of options depending on cost, complexity, and features offered. Users of the video cameras will have a wide range of needs and requirements for the videos they would like to shoot. Purchasing various cameras from basic to high-end instead of one brand and model is an effective way to increase versatility. Instead of purchasing as many of one kind of camera (either high-end or low-end) as your budget will allow, consider purchasing a few from each level. Then, after a period of time, an assessment of use and need can help determine which brands or types of cameras best fit your program and whether additional purchases are warranted. Following is additional information regarding low-end and high-end camera options.

### Low-End Features

A low-end, inexpensive camera is useful to those users who do not want or do not require a higher level of settings, such as manual control of shutter speed, aperture, or audio recording levels, or even the highest video quality. Rather, they may only need a simple device to record an event. Cameras that fall into this category include most point-and-shoot cameras with video recording capabilities. Even a smartphone (iPhone or Android device) could be considered a low-end video camera. Following are some of the examples of features users like in these types of cameras.

**Ease of use.** Many users want a camera that is simple to turn on and to maneuver through options, settings, and modes. Most basic cameras have an automatic setting that will allow the user to turn the camera on and hit a red record button. This will reduce common questions, for those users generally do not have much experience with technology or digital devices.

**File export.** Most users understand the process of recording video but forget to consider the process of moving the files from the camera to a computer or other device. These cameras generally provide options for a file format that is easy to edit (if needed) or is easy to export to a common web-friendly format such as .mov, .mp4, or .avi.

**Cost.** Basic cameras will cost less and allow for the purchase of more cameras overall.

### High-End Features

The following features and settings are generally included in the purchase of higher-end or prosumer-level video cameras, such as a Nikon or Canon DSLR or Blackmagic Cinema Camera:

**White-balancing options.** This allows for color correction in different lighting environments so that the overall image does not look too orange or blue.

**External microphone input.** This is the ability to add a microphone to the video camera other than the one built in.

**Headphone input.** This allows the user to listen to the audio and monitor the volume levels in real time to know what will be recorded.

**Shoe adapter.** This allows for common mounting of microphones and lights.

**Usage.** It is important to consider what kinds of videos users need to shoot with this equipment. Is the purpose to record interviews, studio shoots, outdoor video, or indoor video? These questions will help determine what type of video camera you purchase and whether you need basic cameras or higher-end cameras.

**Resolution and file format of video.** Most high-end cameras will record a resolution of 1080p, and newer cameras have the ability to record to 4K (more than double 1080p in terms of lines of resolution). Look for a recorded-video file format that works effectively with the editing system being used or final output required by those using the video cameras. This can be determined by looking at the manual of the video-editing software provided to determine supported video formats.

**Lenses.** Some video cameras will have the ability to use interchangeable lenses. This great feature brings an added versatility to the cameras and the possibility of enhanced shooting situations. Telephoto lenses (100–300 mm) are available for long-range shooting, while wide-angle lenses are good for wide shots and landscapes (12–35 mm).

## Video Accessories

In addition to acquiring digital still and video cameras, you will need to have on hand various accessories that patrons can check out to enhance their video projects, such as tripods, light kits, extra lenses, and cables. Figure 3.6 provides an image of some of these, and they are discussed below.

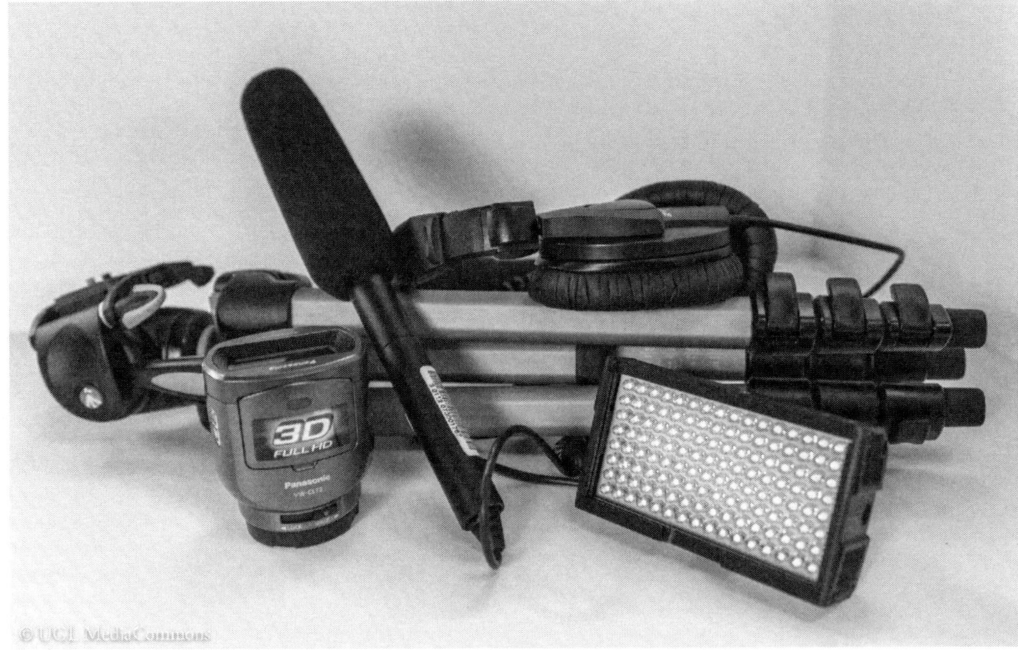


**Figure 3.6.** Image of Video Accessories

**Tripods.** To avoid the "shaky cam" feel, tripods are essential for almost any video shoot. Based on experience from the UIUC program, look for tripods with mostly metal parts. Tripods with plastic parts in key areas can easily break. The metal tripods purchased as replacements cost approximately 10–20 percent more but have lasted much longer than the originals, justifying the cost.

**Portable light kits.** Lighting can be an issue if most video shoots are held indoors, especially in low-light or fluorescent-lighting situations. Small battery-powered lights are simple to use and add a basic studio-lighting feel to the video. Some recommendations for lighting kits include:

- Helios 3-Point Lighting Kit: http://gear.digitaljuice.com/products/products.asp?pid=2404
- LimoStudio: http://www.amazon.com/LimoStudio-Photography-Portrait-Umbrella-Continuous-Lighting/dp/B005FHZ2SI/ref=sr_1_1?ie=UTF8&qid=1398785543&sr=8-1&keywords=lighting+kit
- Lowel lighting kits: http://www.lowel.com/kits.html

**Microphones.** Microphones built into most video cameras are omnidirectional and will record a large amount of environmental noise along with the subject of the audio. External shotgun and lavalier microphones allow for higher-quality audio recordings in most environments and situations. For example, if a user is conducting a simple interview, he or she can use a wired or wireless lavalier microphone that places the microphone itself close to the mouth of the person speaking and minimizes environmental noise. An entry-level consumer wired lavalier set can be purchased for less than twenty dollars. Figure 3.7 illustrates the addition of some of these accessories to a camera.

**Figure 3.7.** Image of High-End Camera, External Lavalier Mic, and Light Added to a Camera

**Memory cards.** Many cameras will include some built-in memory and a slot for memory cards. It is useful to have some memory cards available to users as well as a smart-card reader for easy transfer from card to computer. You may want to purchase various cards with capacities ranging from 8–32 GB. The size of the card needed depends on the resolution of the video being recorded and the average length of the shoot. For example, a 1080p video file will consume approximately 10–20 Mbps (Megabits per second) depending on the quality. So every minute of video would be 600 Mb–1.2 Gb.

## Backpocket Kits (Accessories for Modern Smartphones)

Most modern smartphones, whether running Android or iOS, have a fairly decent still and video camera. Most are capable of shooting 1080p (high definition) video and large-resolution still images. For users, the smartphone also has the added benefit of familiarity. Owners should understand how to operate the applications and may even know how to get the videos and photos off the camera. Smartphones have just a few weak points (form factor that is tough to keep still, poor audio recording quality) that keep them from really producing quality video; luckily these can be improved with simple low-cost accessories, such as the following:

**External microphones.** As with standard video cameras, the downside of having an onboard microphone on a smartphone is that it introduces environmental noise between the camera and the subject. Most shotgun and lavalier microphones that are purchased for other cameras can also function with most smartphones with the addition of a simple breakout cable. A breakout cable separates the inputs for microphone and audio. Figure 3.8 provides an illustration of a breakout cable attached to a phone.

**Figure 3.8.** Image of Breakout Cable with Smartphone and Mic

**Camera stabilizer (smartphone case).** Holding a smartphone steady for any length of time can be tricky, and most videos over a few seconds in length tend to be "shaky" and "jittery." By using a small camera-stabilizer case for the smartphone, the user has much more control over any camera movements. Some also have the benefit of being able to hold extra microphones and lights. Figure 3.9 is an example of a case for a smartphone.

**Figure 3.9.** Image of DiffCase

You may want to have several backpocket kits in your collection and advertise them as a way to turn patrons' smartphones into higher-end video and digital recording devices. Backpocket kits are significantly less expensive to purchase and can extend your budget while increasing options for patrons. Even with the use of a camera stabilizer, patrons may benefit from checking out a tripod to keep the camera still.

## Product Testing

Ordering one device for testing before making large orders is essential for avoiding poor choices. Even though a piece of equipment looks good on paper, once the item is tested, it may lack something that will make it difficult for users. During testing, remember to think about how a user would operate the device, including how they would potentially get a file off the device and then what they would need to do with the file once off. Also determine how efficiently it would integrate with the current loanable technology processes. The following are additional questions to help guide choice of equipment.

- If the user leaves data on the device, is it easy to delete?
- If the user stays logged into the device, can it be wiped clean without viewing personal data?
- If the device is able to have a password entered, can that be wiped once the device has been returned?
- Are the settings and system menu preferences easy to understand and modify by users of varying levels?
- Will this device require several accessories (such as memory cards, batteries, paid data, or applications) that raise the initial and recurring costs?

When planning the equipment to purchase for a loanable technology program, it is critical to work with an advisory group that is composed of stakeholders and community members invested in the services of the library. They can help guide the process based on a needs assessment (or even help prepare and analyze results from a needs assessment) and consult with others about possible equipment to purchase. The equipment to be purchased will vary from library to library and may even need to be purchased in stages. The advisory group can help in setting a process for selecting and testing the equipment.

## Key Points

The process for deciding on the equipment to purchase for a loanable technology program can be time consuming and will require consultation from experts from various areas. The following points were discussed in this chapter to aid in the process.

- Do some preplanning to have a basic strategy for your equipment purchases, based on results from a needs assessment. A collection development policy will help to guide this process.
- Include your stakeholders in the planning process and in suggestions for equipment purchases.
- Establish early on the specific goals to be accomplished for the program and the program's parameters, such as the audience, acceptable uses (academic, leisure,

etc.), size and scope of the program, and whether items can circulate outside of the library. Investigate the different platforms that are available and make sure you understand the ramifications of providing equipment that requires a personal ID or security imprint.

- Think strategically about the types of equipment to purchase initially. Rather than purchasing many high-end, newer models of equipment, compare the pros and cons of acquiring that equipment versus earlier models or lower-end equipment. Begin with testing various models. After a period, evaluate how the equipment is being used and base your next purchases on usage and need.
- Remember to have on hand the necessary accessories that will augment the quality of the lower-end cameras or even smartphones.

Deciding on equipment to purchase is just one aspect of a loanable technology program. There are other components that need to be included in a budget as well. Those and suggestions for an initial and ongoing budget are discussed in the next chapter.

CHAPTER 4

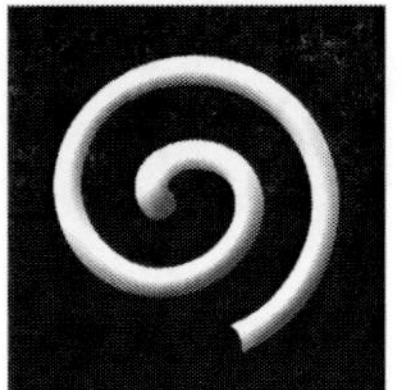

# Budgeting

## IN THIS CHAPTER

- ▷ Determining start-up expenses for a program, including a recommended start-up budget for equipment purchases, storage, replacement and maintenance costs, and other associated costs
- ▷ Planning a budget based on types and numbers of equipment to purchase
- ▷ Determining an ongoing budget
- ▷ Garnering ongoing financial support, including a recommended percentage for ongoing budget allocation

THE LAST CHAPTER PROVIDED details of the process for evaluating new technology items for purchase, but ultimately this will depend upon the needs of your clientele and library budget. Determining a budget for any program takes planning and reassessment as the program evolves. The budget required for a loanable technology program will vary from year to year—more significant in the first year to account for the establishment of a core loanable technology pool and smaller in subsequent years for supplemental items that will round out or replace the original collection.

Planning a budget for a loanable technology program can have multiple stages built in, including initial costs for a program and ongoing costs. The first part of this chapter will provide some recommendations for a start-up budget, followed by suggestions for setting an ongoing budget. Each library will need to determine how much is available for both the initial phase of a program and ongoing costs. Although the initial start-up cost will vary dramatically from one library to the next, table 4.1 provides an example breakdown of percentage recommendations for both start-up and yearly costs for new equipment, packaging and supplies, maintenance and replacement costs, and associated costs.

**Table 4.1.** Start-Up and Yearly Loanable Technology Budget Recommended by Percentages

| | SHARE OF START-UP BUDGET (%) | BREAKDOWN OF $10,000 START-UP BUDGET ($) | SHARE OF YEARLY BUDGET (%) | BREAKDOWN OF $2,000 YEARLY BUDGET ($) |
|---|---|---|---|---|
| New equipment | 70 | 7,000 | 65 | 1,300 |
| Packaging and supplies | 10 | 1,000 | 18 | 360 |
| Maintenance/replacement | 7 | 700 | 7 | 140 |
| Associated costs | 13 | 1,300 | 10 | 200 |
| Storage cabinets (2) | 10.0 | 1,000 | | |
| File cabinet (1) | 2.5 | 250 | | |
| Office supplies | 0.5 | 50 | | |
| Total | 100 | 10,000 | 100 | 2,000 |

## Start-Up Budget

The start-up costs for a loanable technology program can be fairly significant, depending on the scope of your program and how many physical resources are already available. Equipment is probably the first thing that comes to mind when thinking about fund allocation for a loanable technology program. However, other items that need to be purchased or repurposed prior to purchasing equipment include equipment storage, file storage, and packaging for equipment and peripherals. A more specific breakdown of the start-up budget categories is included at the end of each of the following sections. Each of the categories is meant to be a recommendation that can be adjusted based on individual library situations.

### Equipment

The process of determining which equipment to purchase should be based on the needs assessment, which, as described in chapter 2, can be accomplished with both formal and informal approaches, such as surveys, polls, usage statistics, interviews, focus groups, and discussions. After the results are analyzed, a plan can be prepared for what to purchase, probably over a number of years, depending on allocation of funds. The initial phase of equipment purchasing might include buying basic cameras, tablets, laptops, graphing calculators, e-readers, voice recorders, cables, chargers, and items that surfaced in the needs assessment as most critical or that were most frequently asked for by patrons. As a program evolves, again based on assessment of needs and usage statistics, you might decide to purchase higher-end equipment. At some point, a collection development policy should be created to help guide purchases. This is discussed more in chapter 7.

### Quantity and Models to Purchase

Using cameras as an example, the following questions are some you might think about when deciding how many items and which models to purchase:

- Does your budget allow you to purchase all the cameras in your plan the first year or do you need to spread out purchases over a number of years? Keep in mind that a model may no longer be available in subsequent years, or a newer model may be available, but with different functionality. If the goal is to acquire a certain number of cameras of the same model (for ease of use and continuity for patrons), you may want to purchase them all together. That may mean delaying the purchase of other items.
- Did your needs assessment reveal that a basic camera is sufficient for patron use (such as a point-and-shoot model)? Was there evidence that a middle- or high-end camera was needed? If there was enough demand for a middle- or high-end camera, it might be worthwhile initially to make the bulk of camera purchases for basic cameras and perhaps purchase one middle- or high-end camera to test it out with patrons for functionality and use. If the model that was purchased is determined to be the appropriate model, you can buy more as needed. If not, you can explore other options.
- Do you want to purchase the extended warranty on equipment? This is an added cost but with heavy patron use can be beneficial. Make sure to check if the warranty covers damage such as broken doors and lenses on cameras, accidental damage, and other types of damage that might be likely to occur.

The University of Illinois at Urbana-Champaign (UIUC) purchased two Nikon D5200 DSLR cameras. Due to their popularity during the first several months, it was decided to purchase two more. The price had come down a little, but that was because a newer model was being released. In this case, the question was whether or not to purchase the newer model (same price as the older, but different features) or purchase more of the older model that was already in the program. Both of these examples illustrate the importance of planning ahead for purchases based on possible cost fluctuation and changes in features for different models.

In another case, UIUC purchased twenty midrange Panasonic HC-V700M camcorders. About six months after the equipment was purchased, due to the popularity of the items, it was decided to purchase five more. At the time of the second purchase, this particular model of video camera was available from only one vendor and the price was about $120 more for each camera. Purchasing five additional cameras meant that it was necessary to spend $600 more on the cameras than if they had been purchased all at one time. A recommended budget allocation is listed in textbox 4.1.

Table 4.2 provides a breakdown of types of basic equipment one might purchase, based on the start-up budget presented in table 4.1. The "Quantity" column gives the suggested number of items to purchase; however, this number can easily be adjusted based on a library's needs and budget. The "Price per item" column contains a rounded figure, not

### TEXTBOX 4.1

Spend 60–70 percent of start-up funds for equipment purchases, including shipping costs. The rest of your budget may be needed for storage, packaging, and accessories.

**Table 4.2.** Recommended Equipment for Start-Up Budget

| EQUIPMENT TYPE | QUANTITY | PRICE PER ITEM ($) | TOTAL PER EQUIPMENT TYPE ($) |
|---|---|---|---|
| Midrange camcorders | 5 | 500 | 2,500 |
| Point-and-shoot digital cameras | 10 | 100 | 1,000 |
| Graphing calculators | 3 | 175 | 525 |
| Projectors | 1 | 300 | 300 |
| Scientific calculators | 5 | 10 | 50 |
| Tablets | 3 | 400 | 1,200 |
| Voice recorders | 5 | 100 | 500 |
| Tripods | 5 | 100 | 500 |
| SD memory cards | 5 | 10 | 50 |
| HDMI/VGA cables | 6 | 10 | 60 |
| USB charging cables | 6 | 10 | 60 |
| Apple adapters | 3 | 30 | 90 |
| Headphones | 8 | 20 | 160 |
| **Total** | | | **6,995** |

an actual price, and includes shipping costs. The final column is the sum of the previous two columns, showing how much money is allocated per equipment type.

## Equipment Storage

Equipment storage is dependent on the size and type of equipment to be purchased and the anticipated growth of the collection. Following are some questions to think about related to storage needs:

- How much equipment are you purchasing? Do you anticipate adding to the collection each year or buying the initial equipment and only replacing it every three years or so? This will determine if you need to plan for additional storage for subsequent years or not.
- What are the size differentials for the equipment (many small pieces, or some very tall or large pieces, like tripods)? This will help determine depth and height needed for storage and if you should have moveable shelves.
- What kinds of packaging are you going to use for your equipment, and what are the dimensions? Will the packaging allow the item to stand up (such as in an equipment backpack or case)? Again, this can help determine types of shelving to acquire so that the items can be visible on the shelves and organized in a clear fashion.
- Will you be considering storage cabinets instead of open shelving? If so, where will they be placed? Will they be behind the desk and easily accessible for the staff? Will they need locks? Is there sufficient room for growth?

**Figure 4.1.** Image of Cabinets of Loanable Technology

When planning for tripods, investigate whether or not they will fit in your designated space. Some models do not collapse, which requires them to be stored upright or flat. If the shelves are not deep enough or high enough, this can create difficulties with fitting the tripods into the storage space. If you have adjustable shelves, this might not be a problem. Plan for the growth of the collection and the different sizes of equipment to be stored. Figure 4.1 illustrates how cabinets can be organized to house the equipment.

Cost of cabinets can vary greatly depending on size, material, and whether or not they lock. As an example, $1,000 of the associated costs from table 4.1 is for the purchase of two midrange metal locking cabinets and estimated shipping.

**TEXTBOX 4.2**

Plan to spend about 10 percent of your start-up budget on cabinets for your loanable technology collection if you do not already have these resources available.

## File Storage

File storage is also an important element of initial costs. While you probably will not be keeping a record of what patrons check out after the items have been returned, you may have to keep paper copies of loan agreements, billing records, manuals, and statistics. The cost of filing cabinets and filing supplies are minimal in comparison to everything else you will be purchasing. However, it is important to have these items in place when you start your loanable technology collection. The following questions can help guide decisions for purchasing or repurposing storage furniture:

- Is there a locking file cabinet or desk drawer that can be repurposed, or will you need to purchase one and find a space for this?
- Where will this file cabinet be kept? (Are there institutional privacy rules that dictate where a file cabinet with patron information should be kept?)
- Do you need more than one file drawer or cabinet?

UIUC has items that circulate for one week (for out-of-library use) and two hours (for in-library use only). Each time an item is checked out for one week, an equipment-loan form must be signed and initialed by both the patron and the staff person. These forms get shredded once the item has been returned and checked in and statistical information has been collected. However, until the item is returned and checked to be in good operating order, the form needs to be filed.

If your library uses forms, you will need to decide if you want to use forms that are filled out once a semester, once a year, or every time a patron checks out an item. You may decide to store the one-time agreement forms (such as for laptop use) in a locked file cabinet away from the main circulation area and keep a file cabinet closer to the circulation area for forms that need to be accessed more frequently.

**TEXTBOX 4.3**

Plan to spend about $250 on a file cabinet if you do not already have one to repurpose. This will account for about 2.5 percent of the recommended start-up budget.

## Packaging

Packaging is probably the largest hidden cost in providing a loanable technology pool. Many items will need to have a bag or pouch, as well as barcodes and attached labels. These bags can be costly, especially if not factored into the original budgeting process. The following questions can help guide your choices for packaging.

- Some items will come with their own packaging, but is there a good place on the packaging for you to adhere a label, barcode, or identification tag? As you review items to be purchased, also look at the packaging and plan to purchase alternate packaging, if needed. At times, this will not be obvious until you receive the items.
- Will you use a label machine or tags of some kind? If you use a label machine, remember you will also need supplies.
- Will you want a double barcode or a single? Do you expect each piece of the item to be labeled? If so, do you expect each piece to be labeled with the barcode?
- Will your bags be the same brand across the loanable technology program or will they be unique to the item that is lent?

During the 2012–2013 fiscal year, the UIUC program spent about 10 percent of the loanable technology budget on packaging and other supplies for processing. These included bags, tags, cables, and label tape to package and label all the new items. Table 4.3 shows the types of supplies used for packaging.

**Table 4.3.** Packaging and Supplies

| PACKAGING AND SUPPLIES | QUANTITY | COST PER ITEM ($) | TOTAL COST ($) |
|---|---|---|---|
| Camcorder bags | 5 | 15.00 | 75 |
| Digital camera bags | 10 | 10.00 | 100 |
| Clear bags for calculators, adapters, SD memory cards, voice recorders, and cables | 33 | 5.00 | 165 |
| Bags for headphones | 8 | 12.50 | 100 |
| Tags for external labeling | 50 | 3.50 | 175 |
| Miscellaneous supplies | | | 385 |
| **Total** | | | **1,000** |

The cost of supplies and packaging varies depending on the vendor, the brand, and the quality of the product. Table 4.3 breaks down the start-up budget for packaging and supplies based on the recommended start-up equipment purchase in table 4.1. Miscellaneous supplies could be anything from security tags or strips (such as tattle tape or rfd) to barcodes to label tape and a label-making machine. Figure 4.2 illustrates supplies for packaging.

When UIUC planned for its loanable technology collection, the library invested in different types of bags depending on what type of equipment was going into them. One option is something like a standard black Sumdex 13.3-inch laptop bag for most loanable technology items that could be used outside the library (see figure 4.3). Another is a clear plastic bag (e.g., what is often used for cash handling) for items that are restricted to in-library use only (see figure 4.4). Clear plastic cash-handling bags are good options because it is easy to see the contents of the bag without opening it.

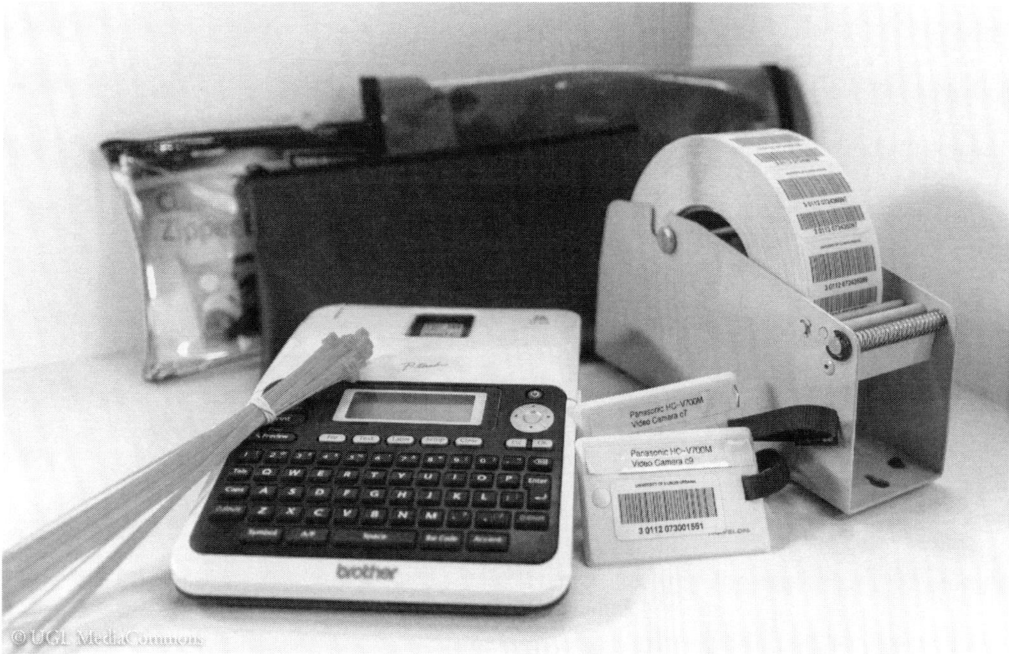


**Figure 4.2.** Supplies for Packaging

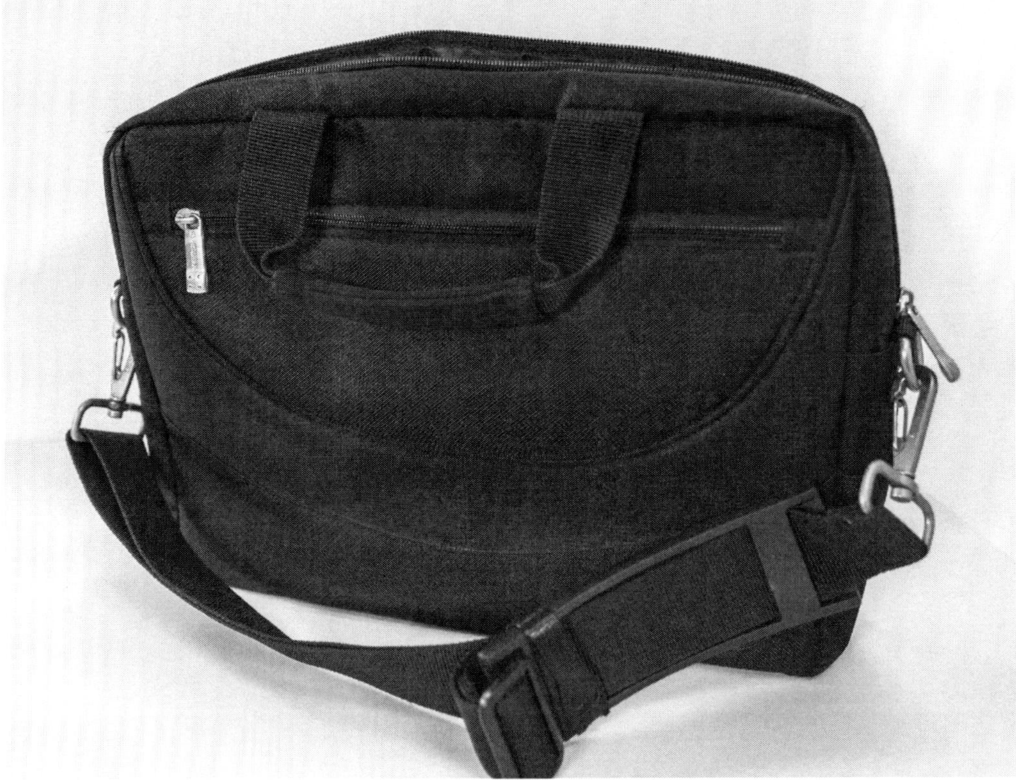

**Figure 4.3.** Picture of Sumdex Bag

As the collection expands for items that can be used outside of the library, you may find that having the same exact bag for many different items can be confusing. If all the packaging is identical, it may be difficult for workers to determine at a glance which item is needed. It is more efficient to have a distinct bag for each item. Distinct could mean a different color of the same bag, a different colored identification tag, or a different style of bag based on the size and type of item being circulated. Figure 4.5 illustrates the organization in the cabinets, and textbox 4.4 provides a recommendation for yearly percentages.

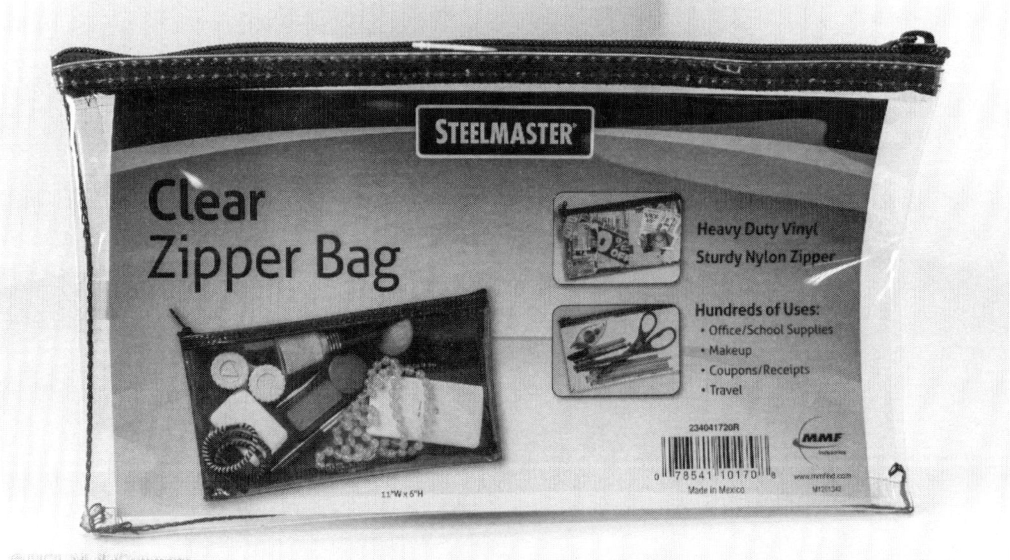


**Figure 4.4.** Picture of Plastic Cash-Handling Bag

**Figure 4.5.** Cabinet Showing Organization of Bags

**TEXTBOX 4.4**

Reserve 10 percent of your start-up budget for packaging.

# Ongoing (Annual) Budget

## Annual Purchase Costs

Ongoing purchase costs will probably be designated to new technology purchases, ongoing warranties, packaging supplies, and replacement items, although sometimes they include annual subscription fees to software programs or other technology support services. Some of this may depend on the allocations that were set up for your program.

For instance, if your institution designates a large amount of money toward the inaugural year of the technology program, it may make sense that many large purchases are made the first year. Subsequent yearly purchases will probably be more supplemental, in an attempt to round out the collection of technology. If there is a core collection of items, it is then possible to purchase accessories that supplement the core collection. Or perhaps the budget includes a three- to five-year replacement cycle for items.

On the other hand, if your institution has designated roughly the same amount in the budget for year-to-year technology acquisitions, it is possible that the first year's budget will go toward a few copies of a diverse range of equipment. Each subsequent year's budget for new technology may include new copies of the equipment, but perhaps not as many supplemental items. It may take longer to develop a core collection and, consequently, a supplemental collection.

As an example of how a budget shifts from the start-up phase to an ongoing phase, in the 2013–2014 fiscal year, UIUC spent 65 percent of its loanable technology budget on new technology purchases. This was down 23 percentage points from the 2012–2013 fiscal year, when 88 percent of the budget was for new technology purchases to support the new media commons. It is common to front-load purchases for a new program. See textbox 4.5 for a recommendation of percentages to spend per year. Figure 4.6 illustrates the shifts in expenses at UIUC over an eight-year period.

**TEXTBOX 4.5**

Once the program is established, allocating 65 percent of the yearly loanable technology budget toward new acquisitions allows you to spend a higher percentage of the budget on maintenance, repair, and supplies. For example, if your yearly loanable technology budget is $2,000, you would spend $1,300 on new acquisitions and have $700 for supplies, replacements, and associated costs.

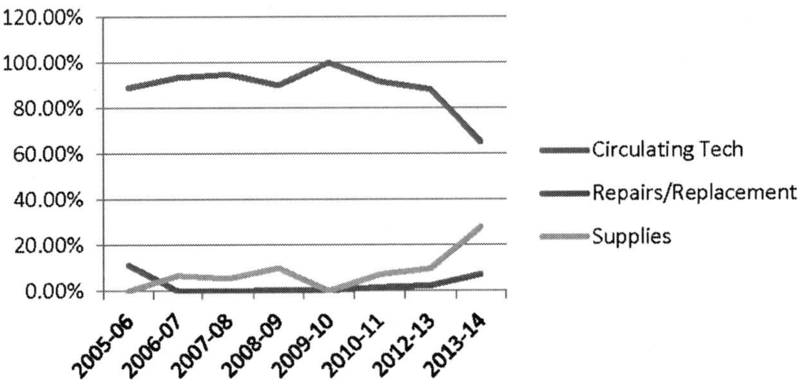


**Figure 4.6.** UIUC Loanable Technology Expenses 2005–2013

## Replacement and Maintenance Costs

Replacement and maintenance costs will probably not be a substantial part of the budget until at least the second year of operation. The first calendar year of having any given item in circulation usually reveals any frequently occurring problems with either the technology itself or the physical casing, both of which are sometimes covered under the warranty. The second year is typically when the need for repairs is noticed. Unless an extended warranty is purchased for technology items, you will need to determine whether to replace the part, purchase a new copy of the same model, or purchase a new copy of a different model of the item. Any option you choose requires spending money. Also keep in mind that the current technology-item life cycle is two to four years.

Again, as an example of the shift that can occur in percentages needed for replacement costs, at UIUC during the 2012–2013 fiscal year, 2 percent of the budget was spent on replacement and maintenance costs. In the first half of the 2013–2014 fiscal year, 7 percent of the budget was spent on replacement and maintenance costs. The percentage increased partly because less was spent on new technology to add to the technology pool, but also because more was spent on repairing or replacing the items that were in circulation. Owing to the opening of the media commons, there are now many more items in the collection, including many high-end items that require replacement or maintenance. For example, one model of a digital camera has a battery door cover that keeps breaking. This piece is not essential, but it does cover the battery and SD card slot. The replacement battery door is only about six dollars, so it is cheaper to continue to replace battery doors instead of purchasing a completely different model of camera.

In another instance, a key piece of a tripod model that had been purchased was plastic and quickly broke. Of the twenty tripods that were originally purchased, only eight remained in the collection a year later. There was no way to repair this piece, so a decision was made to phase out that model of tripod and replace it with a model that included more robust metal pieces in key places. The new model of tripod cost twenty dollars more than the first model that was purchased, but it has withstood rugged use by patrons.

**TEXTBOX 4.6**

Reserve 7 percent of the yearly budget for maintenance costs.

## Associated Costs

Associated costs include the taxes (unless you provide your tax-free number) and shipping added to the order upon purchase. Failure to figure these into your budget could result in a larger than expected total cost. Some items will be cheaper when bought in bulk. It may be more cost effective to purchase particular items (e.g., headphone cables or y-splitters) in a larger quantity if they might be frequent purchases instead of purchasing them periodically and paying the extra shipping and handling each time.

**TEXTBOX 4.7**

Plan to spend 10 percent of the yearly budget on associated costs.

## Donations of Equipment

Occasionally patrons may want to donate equipment to the library, including gently used equipment, older models, or replacements for lost or damaged items they had checked out. It is a good idea to have a policy and process in place before you begin accepting donated equipment. This policy and the process for acceptance could be similar to the process you have for book donations, but it could include a statement about the age and condition of the item being donated. Donations will probably need to be reviewed on a case-by-case basis. You might ask the following questions when drafting an equipment-donation policy:

- Will you accept only new-in-box (NIB) condition? If not, under what circumstances will you accept other technology?
- When will you accept different models of items already in circulation (if at all)?
- How new does the technology need to be in order to add it to the circulation pool? Does it depend on the type of technology donated?

Although it may be appealing to receive "free" materials, keep in mind there are additional costs. In the long run, it could cost more if new cataloging records need to be set up, different packaging needs to be acquired, and additional instructions and new web page entries need to be created. If the item does not complement what is being offered, it may not be worth the extra cost and effort to accept it. It could also be frustrating to patrons and staff to have many variations of a type of technology instead of a consistent brand and model. Item consistency also minimizes time needed to learn how to use the equipment.

Patron donations differ from donations made by departments, teachers, businesses, or community groups, which are given for particular purposes or to support specific classes; however, all these types of donations can be very beneficial to the expansion of the technology pool. Efforts and examples for soliciting these types of donations are further discussed in chapter 7.

## Budget Streams

There are several options for garnering support for a loanable technology program. One of the best options is to build in a percentage of the overall library budget for loanable technology. It may take a few years to determine how much to designate for a loanable technology budget. In the meantime, how does a library get the initial funds for a program? Some of the ways to fund a loanable technology program are from one-time funding allocations, departmental donations, donor funds, and grants.

### One-Time Funds

Once a clear need for the loanable technology program has been determined and a technology plan, vision, and mission statement have been created, then a one-page summary of the program and its needs can be created and distributed to administrators, budget groups (and any finance committees), community groups, the library board, parent-teacher groups (like the Parent Teacher Organization), and others who may have discretionary funds or end-of-year funds available. There may also be opportunities for one-time funds from competitions and from gifts made in memoriam. If there is a process for dissemination of end-of-year funds, it is worth investigating.

Announcements for proposals of competitions to enhance programming periodically appear in newspapers, newsletters, blogs, and district and state organizational correspondence, so it is good to review those. If documents have been prepared that show the need, value, and effect of a loanable technology program for the constituency being served (whether it is students or community patrons), the proposal process can be expedited.

## Donor Funds

Depending on the population served by the library, donations of smaller sums to fulfill specific needs can also be solicited. Communities can be made aware of these needs through newsletters, the library website, signs in the library, and flyers. Many libraries have a newsletter or a wish list, perhaps from the institution's development or advancement office or put out by a "Friends of the Library" group. When gifts are received, make sure to send a personal thank-you note along with information about how the money will be used to buy essential equipment that students or patrons can check out of the library. If possible, include pictures of the item for the donor as well. Donors like to know how their donations are being used, and follow-through with a donor may lead to subsequent gifts.

## Grants

Grants are also available and worth pursuing. There are many resources available for locating grants, but some are specific to type of library, location, or intent. Additionally, some companies might donate equipment to a library. Textbox 4.8 gives some examples of library funding agencies to pursue for possible grants.

### TEXTBOX 4.8

- American Library Association grants page: http://www.ala.org/awards grants/awards/browse/grnt?showfilter=no
- Bill and Melinda Gates Foundation Global Libraries program: http://www.gatesfoundation.org/What-We-Do/Global-Development/Global-Libraries
- Institute of Museums and Library Services (IMLS) Sparks! Ignition Grants for Libraries: http://www.idevmail.net/link.aspx?l=1&d=73&mid=366106&m=1793
- IMLS Library Services and Technology Act Grants to States Program: http://www.imls.gov/programs/
- Laura Bush Foundation for America's Libraries School Library Grant: https://laurabushfoundation.unt.edu/
- Library Grants Center, with categories for national grants (http://salempress.com/store/grants/national_grants.htm) and state grants (http://salempress.com/store/grants/state_grants.htm), as well as a library grants how-to section (http://salempress.com/store/grants/grant_tutorials.htm)

## Ongoing Funds

Once the loanable technology program grows and becomes more established, ongoing, dedicated funding will be needed. Documenting the use of the service is essential. Circulation statistics can help build the case for continued funding and establish the need for a dedicated budget line. If a spreadsheet and ongoing statistics are kept that detail use, instances of unfulfilled requests due to high demand for items, and examples of how the program is helping students or community members in their projects, it becomes easier to advocate for ongoing funding, map out the program, and plan for growth. Gathering patron (or student, teacher, and faculty) stories of how the service has benefited them and obtaining their support to speak on behalf of the program may help in advocating for a dedicated budget line. A reliable budget stream allows for future planning of technology needs for public use.

Unless your library has a large fund from donations or unrestricted funds, it will be important to consider up front how much you can spend on loanable technology items each year. If these funds are not sufficient, then you will need to seek outside sources and also prepare a case to present to your library or school administration, library board, trustees, finance group, budget group, or whoever else is responsible for overall library funding. Your case may involve documents, statistics, and assessments of the service that provide stories from your constituencies about the use, impact, and value of the service.

## Key Points

When determining your start-up budget and ongoing budget, keep the following in mind:

- Remember to allocate part of the start-up budget for replacement parts, equipment storage, file storage, and packaging for equipment and peripherals.
- After the initial year, it will be important to have percentages in mind for budget allocation. Recommended percentages for budget allocation after the initial year might be 65 percent for new equipment, 18 percent for packaging and supplies, 7 percent for maintenance and replacement costs, and 10 percent for associated costs.
- Investigate budget streams such as ongoing funds, one-time funds, donor funds, and opportunities from grant and competition sources.

Just as it is important to establish need and a budget for the loanable technology program, it is equally important to establish consistent practices and policies for how the equipment will handled. Chapter 5 provides suggestions for cataloging the equipment.

# Cataloging Items

**IN THIS CHAPTER**

- ▷ Instances when cataloging might or might not be necessary for loanable technology
- ▷ Types of cataloging formats, records, and best practices for cataloging loanable technology
- ▷ Cataloging tips for creating bibliographic, holdings, and item records for loanable technology items

ONCE NEED FOR A PROGRAM has been determined, a budget established, and the initial equipment evaluated, selected, and purchased, the next step is to think about how to catalog and process the equipment. This chapter will help you determine whether or not your library needs to catalog your items and will present monograph and serials options for creating cataloging records.

## Is Cataloging Loanable Technology Right for Your Library?

Cataloging or not cataloging items directly correlates with circulation policy and procedure, so it is important to keep those in mind when determining a cataloging policy and procedure for your library. Many, though not all, libraries opt to create catalog records for loanable technology items and track the checkout of items through their circulation systems. Depending on the size of the technology collection or value of the individual item, you may decide that it is not necessary to catalog every item. For items that are not cataloged, a paper-and-pen checkout system may work just fine. Some examples include items that are used only within the library, such as inexpensive calculators, USB jump drives, headphones, cables, or phone chargers. For example, you might decide that items costing less than twenty dollars that are used only within the library do not need to be cataloged. Many libraries let patrons borrow these items in exchange for something without which the patron will be inconvenienced—an identification card, a wallet, or even a shoe, for example. This practice varies depending on individual library policy. The solution for one library might not work for other libraries.

There are, however, many benefits to cataloging loanable technology, including: the technology can be viewed in the online catalog; checkout can occur through the circulation system; and statistics can be gathered more easily. Another advantage of adding all items to the online catalog is that it provides consistency in circulation procedures and ease in administering loan periods, renewals, and fines. In most cases, if the equipment is not cataloged, it is too complex and time consuming to track the status of equipment unless the volume of requests is minimal and items are borrowed for in-library use only. Another important reason to include all the loanable technology equipment in the catalog is that the catalog can automatically generate courtesy overdue notices and billing notices. Billing best practices will be discussed in further detail in chapter 10.

**TEXTBOX 5.1**

Cataloging all loanable technology allows patrons to see real-time information about whether or not an item is available.

## Precataloging Questions

The next section will discuss types of cataloging formats, records, and best practices for cataloging loanable technology. However, prior to creating records, you will need to establish parameters for loan periods and renewal options. Below are some questions that you will need to answer for any technology that you will loan out in order to develop consistent policies and procedures. The answers to the questions will be incorporated into the catalog fields that are described in the next sections. What are the loan periods?

- Are there items that can be borrowed only within the library for a few hours?
- Can equipment be renewed?
- If equipment can circulate outside the library, should it circulate for three days, five days, or one or two weeks?
- Should equipment follow the same loan period as media items (such as DVDs or Blu-rays)?
- Are any of your current loan periods or item types applicable or adaptable for loanable technology (e.g., reserve status, book, DVD, etc.)?
- Do loanable technology items need to have a new "item type" in the catalog with distinct rules?
- Are there other library departments, branches, or consortia that use the same library catalog or that acquire and catalog technology items that circulate? If so, individuals responsible for cataloging and maintaining the collection should come to agreement on best practices and suggestions of item types to use, as well as suggestions for headings and fields to use in the records.

## Creating MARC Bibliographic, Holdings, and Item Records

This section provides examples of creating MARC records in the library catalog for loanable technology, which differs from monographs or serials. MARC stands for Machine-Readable Cataloging and is a standard for bibliographic records. As a matter of reference, the Library of Congress has developed a web resource called "Understanding MARC Bibliographic: Machine-Readable Cataloging" (http://www.loc.gov/marc/umb/). It provides an overview of what MARC is and why librarians should use it in cataloging. Also included are explanations of the fields in a MARC record, many of which will be discussed in this chapter.

When cataloging loanable technology, usually a MARC short record can be used. A short record may also be called a "brief" or "basic" record, or some other phrase, but it includes far fewer fields than a full record. The person who catalogs loanable technology will potentially be whoever does monographic cataloging in the library. However, a decision should be made on whether to create a short (basic) or more detailed catalog record. Some of this may depend on how many items are in the loanable technology collection and how similar they are to each other. In a library with a smaller loanable technology collection it may be more advantageous to create shorter records that are more general. In a library that has a large circulating technology collection, it may be more effective to include more details in the record than what are explained here.

For instance, if a library with a small loanable technology collection and a library with a large loanable technology collection both own the same model of Nikon camera, it is likely that the library with the large collection will be more detailed with its catalog records to distinguish between that camera and others it owns—especially if the library circulates other models of Nikon cameras. The library with the larger collection may want to include more information in the title statement to distinguish between its Nikon D5200 and Nikon CoolPix cameras. The smaller library may have only a Nikon D5200, so when a patron walks up to the circulation desk to request "the Nikon camera," it is very clear to which camera they are referring.

**TEXTBOX 5.2**

Libraries with larger loanable technology collections should include more detailed information about the specific model of the item somewhere in the bibliographic record. That way, if the library owns more than one model of one brand (e.g., two different Nikon cameras), the items will be easily distinguishable in the catalog.

### The MARC Bibliographic Record

Before you think about adding another bibliographic record to your catalog, search the catalog to make sure there is not already another of the same item in the catalog. As with monographs, you would not want to have duplicate records for the same edition of an item in the catalog.

There are several ways to input a MARC bibliographic record in your library catalog, whether they are short or full records. The first way is to check OCLC Connexion (connexion.oclc.org)—if your library has a subscription to it—to see if a complete record has already been created. If it has, cataloging becomes much simpler. If so:

- Download the record to the catalog.
- Modify it to desired specifications.
- Add holdings and item records.

If a record cannot be found, or it is preferred to use the uniformity of existing local or original cataloging standards, then you will need to create a bibliographic record from scratch, which is the second method. When you create an original record, you can include as many tags and subfields as desired. For your original record, use at least the following fields in the bibliographic record: 245 (title statement), 246 (varying form of title), and 500, 504, or 520 (general and summary notes fields). The title statement may be a generic form of the title (Panasonic video camera) or a specific title (Panasonic HC-V700M HD camera), but the 246 fields should include as many variations of the title as possible to help patrons searching for an item like this (e.g., video camera, HD camera, camcorder, Panasonic camcorder, Panasonic video camera, Panasonic HD camera, Panasonic camera).

Table 5.1 provides an example of a short MARC bibliographic record created at the University of Illinois at Urbana-Champaign (UIUC) library for a Panasonic HC-V700M HD video camera. Each short bibliographic record includes the following tags: 245 (title statement), 246 (varying form of title), 500 (general note), and 655 (index term—genre/form). Each tag has two indicator fields following it, which further indicate to the machine how to read the record.

### TEXTBOX 5.3

For more information on indicators, please see "MARC Terms and Their Definitions" on the Library of Congress's webpage "What Is a MARC Record and Why Is It Important?" (http://www.loc.gov/marc/umb/um01to06.html#part3).

**Table 5.1.** Example of a MARC Bibliographic Record

| TAG | I1 | I2 | SUBFIELD DATA |
|---|---|---|---|
| 245 | 0 | 0 | ‡a Panasonic HC-V700M HD Camera ‡h [equipment]. |
| 246 | 3 | | ‡a HD video camera. |
| 246 | 3 | | ‡a Camcorders. |
| 246 | 3 | | ‡a Panasonic HD camera. |
| 246 | 3 | | ‡a Panasonic video camera. |
| 246 | 3 | | ‡a Panasonic camcorder. |
| 246 | 3 | | ‡a HD camera. |
| 246 | 3 | | ‡a Camera equipment. |
| 500 | | | ‡a HD video camcorder; tripod available for checkout separately. |
| 655 | | 4 | ‡a Loanable technology. |
| 655 | | 4 | ‡a Camera equipment. |
| 655 | | 4 | ‡a Cameras. |
| 655 | | 4 | ‡a Video cameras. |
| 655 | | 4 | ‡a Camcorders. |
| 655 | | 4 | ‡a Digital Cameras. |

Following is further explanation of the MARC tags, corresponding with table 5.1.

**The 245 tag (see textbox 5.4).** This is used to enter the exact title of the item as it appears on the original packaging. A suggested formula for title statements is brand first, then model, then type of equipment. That way, when patrons find the information in the catalog, they are supplied with specific information about the item, including its current status. The indicators are both zeros in this case (see table 5.1) because there are no added entries and all characters are to be filed. Two subfields are used: ‡a and ‡h. The ‡a subfield is, of course, the title and the ‡h subfield designates the medium, which in this case is "equipment."

**TEXTBOX 5.4**

Use the following formula for 245 title statements: brand, model, then type of equipment (e.g., Lumix ZR1 digital camera).

**The 246 tag (see textbox 5.5).** This is for the "varying form of title" tag. Use as many forms and combinations of the title as are reasonable—both proper and vernacular—to anticipate what any patron might use to search in the catalog. It is OK to retroactively add 246 fields to the bibliographic record to include a search term that a patron has been using unsuccessfully. Three is used as the first indicator in the bibliographic record (no note, added entry), and the second indicator field is left blank because there is no type specified. The only subfield that is included is ‡a, although it is possible to include as many subfields as are necessary.

**TEXTBOX 5.5**

Retroactively add 246 fields to the bibliographic record, if necessary.

**The 500 tag (see textbox 5.6).** This is a general notes field. In this case, it is where you would include a statement about the function or purpose of the item, usually adapted from the item's description on a website. Sometimes information is also included about what other accessories are available for checkout with that item. It may be helpful to use a 504 field to list all the pieces that circulate with the item. That way patrons and staff can see everything that comes with the item by simply looking at the catalog record. This could be useful when checking which cords and adapters come with a projector or whether a camera circulates with batteries, just to name a couple scenarios. There are no indicators to use with this tag and only the ‡a subfield is used.

**TEXTBOX 5.6**

Use a 504 tag to indicate which pieces circulate with the item so that patrons and staff can easily see if batteries or cords are included.

**The 655 tag (see textbox 5.7).** This is an index term for the genre or form of the item. It is filled in by a controlled vocabulary that might be developed in-house. In the case of UIUC, each item in the loanable technology collection has a 655 field of "loanable technology." When that phrase is used in a search of the catalog, all technology items will appear. As the name of the tag suggests, these are broad categories into which each loanable technology item is placed. Most of the time, more than one category applies to each item. These tags also serve as the fields used to populate several internally developed websites that assist with the checkout and reservation process (which will be discussed in more depth in chapter 8). Because the information assists students and staff with information retrieval, it is important to have a controlled vocabulary.

**TEXTBOX 5.7**

Using a controlled vocabulary for the 655 tag will allow patrons to search the online catalog for a specific item category (such as projectors, cameras, or audio devices).

It is not recommended that you export short records to OCLC because they are not complete—especially if the title you are using is not specific to the equipment model you are cataloging.

## The MARC Holdings Record

Three cataloging choices are available when creating the holdings record: single-part, multipart, or serial record.

**Single-part record.** Used for an item that is a single, complete physical entity, like a single DVD, a single-volume monograph, or a technology item that circulates with only one piece. Use this type if you are loaning each piece of an item individually without being packaged together (e.g., a cable, projector, remote control, battery, and instruction manual).

**Multipart record.** Used for an item that has a specified or predetermined number of parts or volumes, like an encyclopedia set, a set of maps, or a technology item that has multiple pieces. If each piece that is housed within the same bag or package gets a separate barcode, the multipart holdings record is probably the best choice.

**Serial record.** An item issued in many parts whose number is not fixed, like a periodical. When cataloging technology items, use this type of holdings record if the same barcode number will be used for each of the pieces that circulates with the main item.

Cataloging technology items can be confusing because none of the options for holdings records is a perfect fit. Each option needs to be modified slightly to apply to technology items. Regardless of the option you choose, make sure the tags used in the holdings record comply with MARC 21 standards.

**TEXTBOX 5.8**

Be consistent in holdings records. It is not recommended to use a combination of single-part, multipart, and serial records when cataloging the loanable technology collection. Use either single-part and multipart records for everything, or serial records for everything.

## Example of a Serial Holdings Record

UIUC uses serial holdings records for the entirety of its loanable technology collection—even the items that have only one piece. The same barcode is used for each piece of the item so that when patrons check out a camera with eight pieces, they have only one item checked out to them instead of eight separate items. This does raise issues from time to time when an item is returned without one of its pieces. Those situations will be discussed in further depth in chapters 8 and 9.

The holdings records are basic—852 for the location, 853 for captions and patterns, and 863 for enumeration and chronology tags. Table 5.2 is an example of a holdings record for the Panasonic HC-V700M HD Camera. Following is an explanation of tags in a serial holdings record:

**The 852 tag.** This is the location tag. It has a first indicator of 7 to denote that the classification and shelving scheme will be specified in ‡2. There is no second indicator, meaning that there is no information provided for the shelving order. The rest of the tag consists of subfields ‡b, ‡h, and ‡i (‡2 is not actually used because there is no specified shelving order for loanable technology). Subfield ‡b indicates the sublocation or collection, which in UIUC's case is Undergraduate Loanable Technology and has the code "ugtec." Subfield ‡h indicates the classification part, or the first part of the call number, which for UIUC is TECHLOAN. Finally, subfield ‡i contains the rest of the call number, usually shortened from the title of the item.

**The 853 tag.** This is for captions and patterns—basic bibliographic unit information. The first indicator used is 2 to denote that the field can contract or expand. The second indicator used is 3 to denote that the captions are unverified and all levels may not be present. Subfield ‡8 is used with an entry of 1 to link the information in the 853 field to the information in the tag 863 fields and subfield ‡a with an entry of "c." to depict the first level of enumeration (which is copy number).

**The 863 tag.** This is for the basic bibliographic enumeration and chronology information that links with the information in tag 852. The first indicator of 4 shows holdings level 4 and the second indicator is 0, denoting that the field is compressed. Again, using subfields ‡8 and ‡a links the information to tag 852. In subfield ‡8, the entry is always "1.n0": a number 1 to the left of the decimal, the copy number "n" to the immediate right of the decimal, and a "0" to the immediate right of the copy number.

## Creating Suppressed Holdings Records

When you start a loanable technology collection, you should also plan for the inevitable time when equipment needs to be withdrawn from the collection, when it is no longer functioning or useful. Libraries that are allowed to delete records will not need to create a suppressed holdings record unless for some reason they want an item available for circulation but not searchable in the public catalog. Other libraries may decide they always want to keep a record in the catalog of materials they have purchased, regardless of status (e.g., withdrawn, lost, or missing). For those libraries, the original record could simply be suppressed. When an item is withdrawn, it should be relinked to the suppressed holdings record, thus excluding it as a result in a catalog search. Suppressed holdings records will be necessary only for institutions that do not delete any item records from their system.

**Table 5.2.** Example of a Serial Holdings Record

| TAG | I1 | I2 | SUBFIELD DATA |
|---|---|---|---|
| 852 | 7 | | ‡b ugtec ‡h TECHLOAN ‡i PanasonicVidCam |
| 853 | 2 | 3 | ‡8 1 ‡a c. |
| 863 | 4 | 0 | ‡8 1.10 ‡a 1 |
| 863 | 4 | 0 | ‡8 1.20 ‡a 2 |
| 863 | 4 | 0 | ‡8 1.30 ‡a 3 |
| 863 | 4 | 0 | ‡8 1.40 ‡a 4 |
| 863 | 4 | 0 | ‡8 1.50 ‡a 5 |
| 863 | 4 | 0 | ‡8 1.60 ‡a 6 |
| 863 | 4 | 0 | ‡8 1.70 ‡a 7 |
| 863 | 4 | 0 | ‡8 1.80 ‡a 8 |
| 863 | 4 | 0 | ‡8 1.90 ‡a 9 |
| 863 | 4 | 0 | ‡8 1.100 ‡a 10 |
| 863 | 4 | 0 | ‡8 1.110 ‡a 11 |
| 863 | 4 | 0 | ‡8 1.120 ‡a 12 |
| 863 | 4 | 0 | ‡8 1.130 ‡a 13 |
| 863 | 4 | 0 | ‡8 1.140 ‡a 14 |
| 863 | 4 | 0 | ‡8 1.150 ‡a 15 |
| 863 | 4 | 0 | ‡8 1.160 ‡a 16 |
| 863 | 4 | 0 | ‡8 1.170 ‡a 17 |
| 863 | 4 | 0 | ‡8 1.180 ‡a 18 |
| 863 | 4 | 0 | ‡8 1.190 ‡a 19 |
| 863 | 4 | 0 | ‡8 1.200 ‡a 20 |
| 863 | 4 | 0 | ‡8 1.210 ‡a 21 |
| 863 | 4 | 0 | ‡8 1.220 ‡a 22 |
| 863 | 4 | 0 | ‡8 1.230 ‡a 23 |
| 863 | 4 | 0 | ‡8 1.240 ‡a 24 |
| 863 | 4 | 0 | ‡8 1.250 ‡a 25 |

For instance, if an institution initially has ten pairs of headphones and, two years later, one of them breaks, that item will need to be withdrawn or suppressed from the catalog. Otherwise the catalog will display false information about how many pairs are available. Some libraries might just delete the record, but if there is a practice never to delete a record (for historical record-keeping and research purposes), then it can be suppressed.

The suppressed holdings record structure should be identical to the holdings record structure. If the holdings record used single-part, multipart, or serials cataloging, everything will be the same in the suppressed holdings record—except for the location,

**Table 5.3.** Example of Suppressed Holdings Record

| TAG | I1 | I2 | SUBFIELD DATA |
|---|---|---|---|
| 852 | 7 | | ‡b wdn-nc ‡h TECHLOAN ‡i PanasonicVidCam |
| 853 | 2 | 3 | ‡8 1 ‡a c. |
| 863 | 4 | 0 | ‡8 1.10 ‡a c.1 |

which will be "withdrawn" or whatever designated term indicates that an item is not available. When the physical item in hand is withdrawn, it should be relinked from the active holdings record to the suppressed holdings record so that there is a record of what happened to it in the catalog. Make sure that it is not found if searched for in patron view in the library catalog. The 863 tag line should then be cut from the active holdings record and pasted into the suppressed holdings record so that both holdings records are accurate. Table 5.3 is an example of a suppressed holdings record for a Panasonic HC-V700M HD camera.

**TEXTBOX 5.9**

Check with your cataloging department to see if suppressed holdings records are an option for your library.

## The Item Record

The item record includes information that describes if the item is part of a collection, whether the item will be in a temporary location, how long it circulates, the barcode for the item, how many pieces it has, and the replacement cost. Much of this information is theoretically determined when you develop your policies (as discussed in chapter 7), but the item record is where you apply the policies to the items. Item records are the last of the records to be created. A separate item record should be created for each copy of the item being circulated. The record should be linked to the holdings record that is active, which should autopopulate the location fields when it is created. The look of the item record may vary depending on the integrated library system being used, but the information required for a complete record is very similar. As with the bibliographic record, enter as much information as is appropriate for the library. Figure 5.1 provides an example of an item record.

At UIUC the location of loanable technology items is "Undergraduate Loanable Technology," which is autopopulated when an item record is created and linked to the appropriate holdings record. Following are additional details about the process and the record, as shown in figure 5.1:

- The barcode and copy number are assigned at this time.
- Replacement costs are added at this point. Further discussion of setting replacement costs is provided in chapter 7.
- The number of pieces that will circulate with the main item is added. Usually this is determined prior to the start of cataloging but made official when entered into the item record. Determining which pieces will circulate with the item usually de-

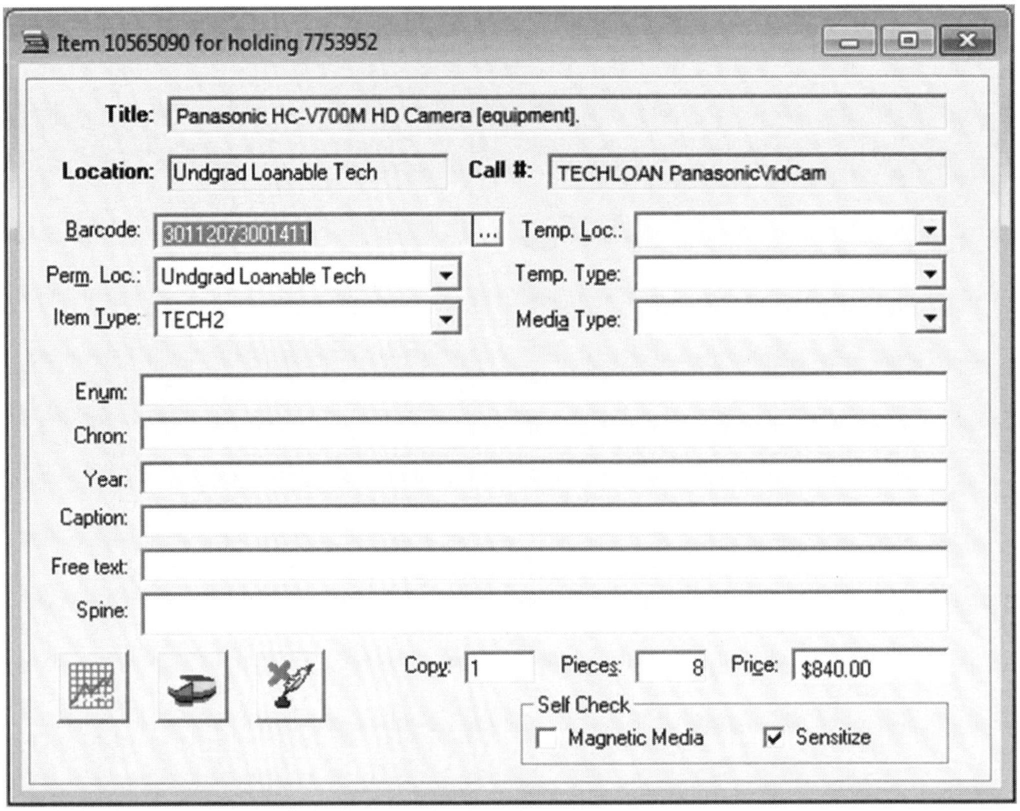

**Figure 5.1.** Example of an Item Record

pends on what is essential for the function of the item. This varies widely depending on the item; for example, video cameras circulate with more pieces than voice recorders. Some items that might be included with a video camera are: instruction sheets (quick-start guide) or manual; cables to connect the camera to a television or other device; or any other commonly needed accessories, such as mics, lights, or batteries. Figure 5.2 shows an example of a record that includes multiple items cataloged with one record.

The cataloging process is complete once the MARC bibliographic records and the serial holdings records are created. Cataloging loanable technology items can be tricky because they are different from monograph or serial items, so it may take awhile to determine what should be the consistent entries in the records. With additional acquisition of equipment, a review of these records will be needed and potential adjustments made to categories, item types, loan periods, and costs.

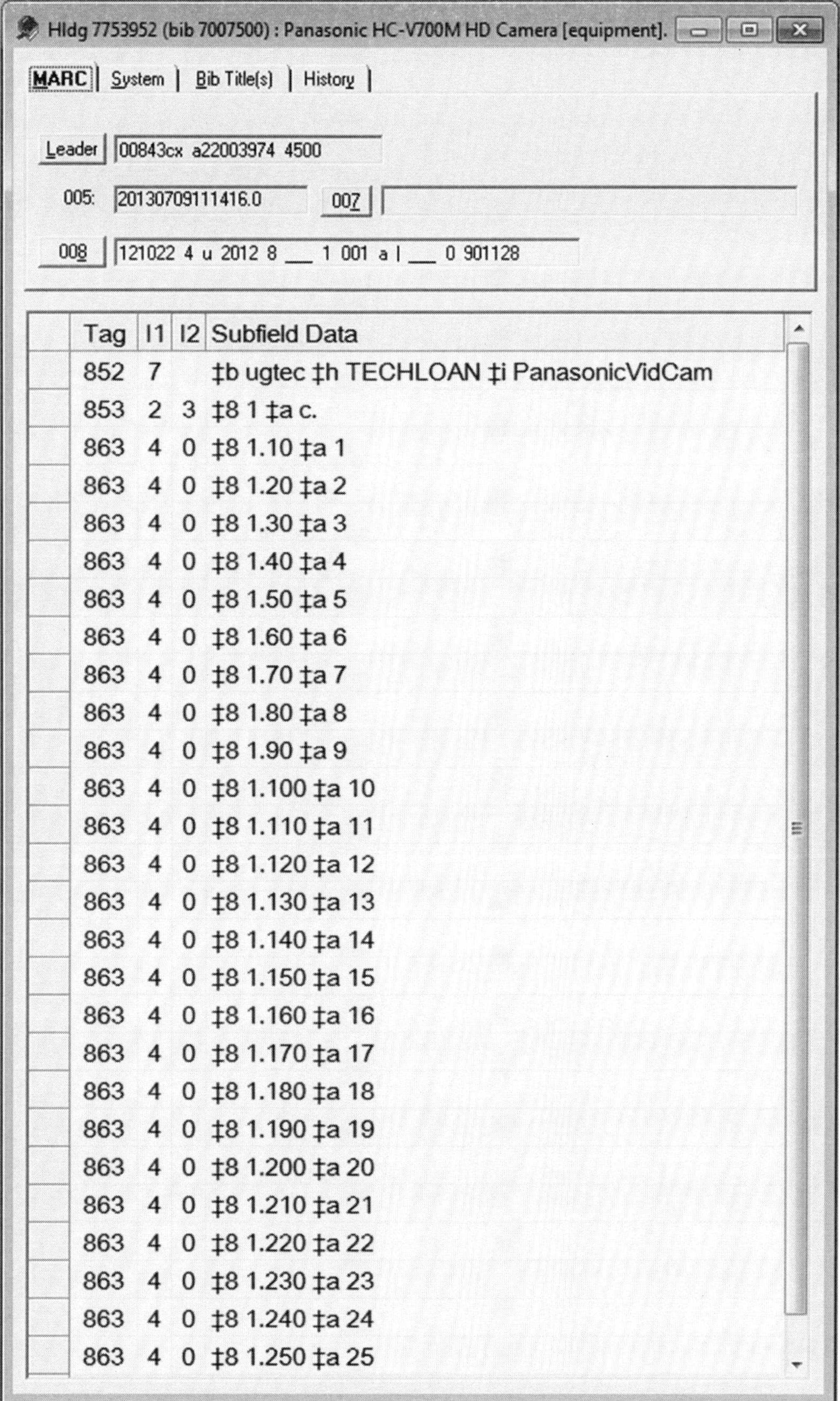
Hldg 7753952 (bib 7007500) : Panasonic HC-V700M HD Camera [equipment].

MARC | System | Bib Title(s) | History

Leader 00843cx a22003974 4500

005: 20130709111416.0 007

008 121022 4 u 2012 8 __ 1 001 a l __ 0 901128

| Tag | I1 | I2 | Subfield Data |
|---|---|---|---|
| 852 | 7 | | ‡b ugtec ‡h TECHLOAN ‡i PanasonicVidCam |
| 853 | 2 | 3 | ‡8 1 ‡a c. |
| 863 | 4 | 0 | ‡8 1.10 ‡a 1 |
| 863 | 4 | 0 | ‡8 1.20 ‡a 2 |
| 863 | 4 | 0 | ‡8 1.30 ‡a 3 |
| 863 | 4 | 0 | ‡8 1.40 ‡a 4 |
| 863 | 4 | 0 | ‡8 1.50 ‡a 5 |
| 863 | 4 | 0 | ‡8 1.60 ‡a 6 |
| 863 | 4 | 0 | ‡8 1.70 ‡a 7 |
| 863 | 4 | 0 | ‡8 1.80 ‡a 8 |
| 863 | 4 | 0 | ‡8 1.90 ‡a 9 |
| 863 | 4 | 0 | ‡8 1.100 ‡a 10 |
| 863 | 4 | 0 | ‡8 1.110 ‡a 11 |
| 863 | 4 | 0 | ‡8 1.120 ‡a 12 |
| 863 | 4 | 0 | ‡8 1.130 ‡a 13 |
| 863 | 4 | 0 | ‡8 1.140 ‡a 14 |
| 863 | 4 | 0 | ‡8 1.150 ‡a 15 |
| 863 | 4 | 0 | ‡8 1.160 ‡a 16 |
| 863 | 4 | 0 | ‡8 1.170 ‡a 17 |
| 863 | 4 | 0 | ‡8 1.180 ‡a 18 |
| 863 | 4 | 0 | ‡8 1.190 ‡a 19 |
| 863 | 4 | 0 | ‡8 1.200 ‡a 20 |
| 863 | 4 | 0 | ‡8 1.210 ‡a 21 |
| 863 | 4 | 0 | ‡8 1.220 ‡a 22 |
| 863 | 4 | 0 | ‡8 1.230 ‡a 23 |
| 863 | 4 | 0 | ‡8 1.240 ‡a 24 |
| 863 | 4 | 0 | ‡8 1.250 ‡a 25 |

**Figure 5.2.** Example of Record with Multiple Items

## Key Points

Cataloging is a technical but important step in the process of getting items ready to circulate. If done thoroughly it can lay the groundwork for a smoothly functioning loanable technology program.

- Some bibliographic records can be downloaded from OCLC Connexion, but they can also be original to your library.
- Consistency in holdings records is important: choose single-part, multipart, or serials cataloging for your technology collection.
- Item records contain important information about a particular copy of equipment, including the barcode, replacement cost, loan period, and number of pieces that circulate.
- For library-specific policies and practices, like cataloging standards, loan periods, deletion or suppression of records, and use of equipment-loan forms, consult with colleagues who are familiar with the population you serve.

In addition to being consistent and thorough with cataloging, it is also critical to take extreme care with how the equipment is processed, packaged, labeled, and housed. This is discussed in the next chapter.

CHAPTER 6

# Processing, Packaging, and Housing Loanable Technology

**IN THIS CHAPTER**

- ▷ How to create and maintain equipment inventory
- ▷ Strategies for choosing packaging (size, color, durability, plastic, cloth, handles, brand, method of closing, and cost) for types of equipment
- ▷ Methods for labeling the item and the package (tags, colors, and information to include)
- ▷ Tips for organizing and labeling the cabinets that have been purchased and put in place for the equipment

THE NEXT STEP IN GETTING the loanable technology items ready to circulate is thinking through how they will be processed, inventoried, packaged, and housed.

## Using a Checklist

Because there is much more involved in the whole process of obtaining, inventorying, cataloging, processing, and preparing loanable technology items than for a single monograph, a checklist should be created to accompany the item until it is completely processed. This is especially important if there are multiple people preparing the item for circulation, since the checklist facilitates communication between staff members who participate in the processing. Figure 6.1 provides a sample checklist.

New Loanable Technology Checklist:

New item: ______________________ Date acquired: ____________

- ☐ Take picture of item + accessories
- ☐ Test item to make sure it works properly
- ☐ Make Contents sheet
- ☐ Sticker the item
  - ○ Loanable Tech sticker
  - ○ 2 hr or 1 wk sticker
- ☐ Package
  - ○ Name label
  - ○ 2 hr or 1 wk sticker
  - ○ Barcode
  - ○ Loanable tech sticker
  - ○ Do not Put in Drop Box sticker
- ☐ Catalog
  - ○ Bib
  - ○ MFHD
  - ○ Items
- ☐ Equipment Loan Form
- ☐ Update Loanable Technology Cabinet Signs
- ☐ Update Loanable Technology Binder
- ☐ Send email to webmaster if necessary
- ☐ Send staff email if necessary
- ☐ Do staff/SA demonstration

**Figure 6.1.** Checklist for New Loanable Technology Spreadsheet

## Inventory Spreadsheet

Inventorying equipment is a step in the process of preparing technology for circulation. It is important to have a centralized location for all equipment records. In some libraries, all technology equipment information will be kept with an information technology department, but the library should also keep an inventory list that includes serial and model numbers of all loanable technology in case of theft or loss.

Information to include in an inventory record would be anything that might help identify the item. This includes serial numbers, model numbers, bar codes, anything that is unique about that particular item, and any institutional markings that have been attached to it. You could create a database for this, but a multipage spreadsheet or simple Microsoft Access database would also work. Figures 6.2 and 6.3 are examples of how to keep inventory in a spreadsheet. Figure 6.2 is an example of a table of contents, and figure 6.3 is an example of an individual item on a page of the spreadsheet.

Figure 6.3 shows a different tab for each category of item. The tabs and the table of contents are hyperlinked within the document for easy navigation. It is a basic spreadsheet created in Microsoft Excel, but the information gathered can be invaluable in order to identify serial numbers or other important information in case of a stolen or missing item.

## Processing the Items for Circulation

As with anything a library owns, an equipment item must have proper identification on it before it can be circulated. This section will give specific examples of how to label circulating equipment and how to create an equipment-loan form.

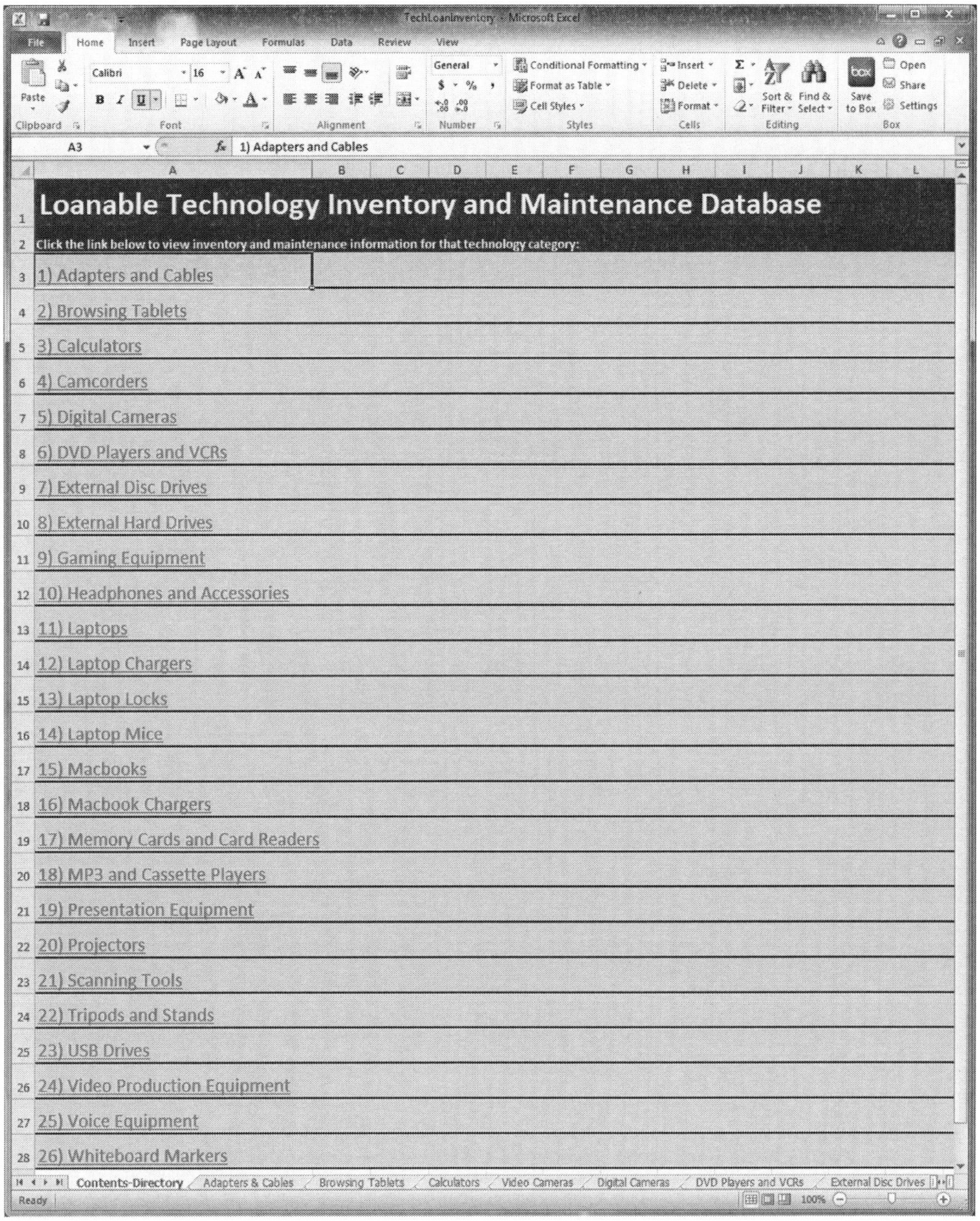
TechLoanInventory - Microsoft Excel
File
Home
Insert
Page Layout
Formulas
Data
Review
View
Paste
Clipboard
Calibri
16
Font
Alignment
General
Number
Conditional Formatting
Format as Table
Cell Styles
Styles
Insert
Delete
Format
Cells
Sort & Filter
Find & Select
Editing
Save to Box
Open
Share
Settings
Box
A3
1) Adapters and Cables
Loanable Technology Inventory and Maintenance Database
Click the link below to view inventory and maintenance information for that technology category:
1) Adapters and Cables
2) Browsing Tablets
3) Calculators
4) Camcorders
5) Digital Cameras
6) DVD Players and VCRs
7) External Disc Drives
8) External Hard Drives
9) Gaming Equipment
10) Headphones and Accessories
11) Laptops
12) Laptop Chargers
13) Laptop Locks
14) Laptop Mice
15) Macbooks
16) Macbook Chargers
17) Memory Cards and Card Readers
18) MP3 and Cassette Players
19) Presentation Equipment
20) Projectors
21) Scanning Tools
22) Tripods and Stands
23) USB Drives
24) Video Production Equipment
25) Voice Equipment
26) Whiteboard Markers
Contents-Directory
Adapters & Cables
Browsing Tablets
Calculators
Video Cameras
Digital Cameras
DVD Players and VCRs
External Disc Drives
Ready
100%

**Figure 6.2.** Screenshot of Inventory Spreadsheet Table of Contents

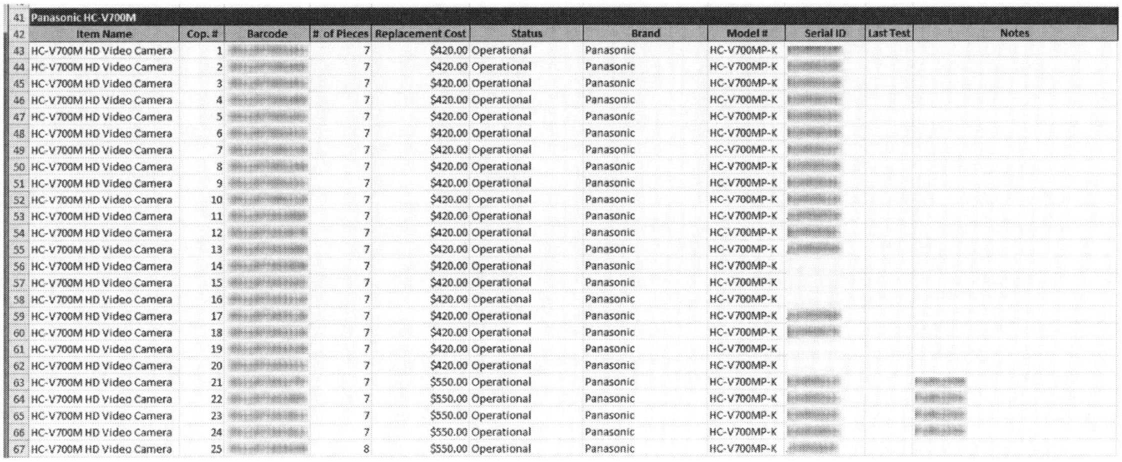

| 41 | Panasonic HC-V700M | | | | | | | | | | |
|---|---|---|---|---|---|---|---|---|---|---|---|
| 42 | Item Name | Cop. # | Barcode | # of Pieces | Replacement Cost | Status | Brand | Model # | Serial ID | Last Test | Notes |
| 43 | HC-V700M HD Video Camera | 1 | [illegible] | 7 | $420.00 | Operational | Panasonic | HC-V700MP-K | [illegible] | | |
| 44 | HC-V700M HD Video Camera | 2 | [illegible] | 7 | $420.00 | Operational | Panasonic | HC-V700MP-K | [illegible] | | |
| 45 | HC-V700M HD Video Camera | 3 | [illegible] | 7 | $420.00 | Operational | Panasonic | HC-V700MP-K | [illegible] | | |
| 46 | HC-V700M HD Video Camera | 4 | [illegible] | 7 | $420.00 | Operational | Panasonic | HC-V700MP-K | [illegible] | | |
| 47 | HC-V700M HD Video Camera | 5 | [illegible] | 7 | $420.00 | Operational | Panasonic | HC-V700MP-K | [illegible] | | |
| 48 | HC-V700M HD Video Camera | 6 | [illegible] | 7 | $420.00 | Operational | Panasonic | HC-V700MP-K | [illegible] | | |
| 49 | HC-V700M HD Video Camera | 7 | [illegible] | 7 | $420.00 | Operational | Panasonic | HC-V700MP-K | [illegible] | | |
| 50 | HC-V700M HD Video Camera | 8 | [illegible] | 7 | $420.00 | Operational | Panasonic | HC-V700MP-K | [illegible] | | |
| 51 | HC-V700M HD Video Camera | 9 | [illegible] | 7 | $420.00 | Operational | Panasonic | HC-V700MP-K | [illegible] | | |
| 52 | HC-V700M HD Video Camera | 10 | [illegible] | 7 | $420.00 | Operational | Panasonic | HC-V700MP-K | [illegible] | | |
| 53 | HC-V700M HD Video Camera | 11 | [illegible] | 7 | $420.00 | Operational | Panasonic | HC-V700MP-K | [illegible] | | |
| 54 | HC-V700M HD Video Camera | 12 | [illegible] | 7 | $420.00 | Operational | Panasonic | HC-V700MP-K | [illegible] | | |
| 55 | HC-V700M HD Video Camera | 13 | [illegible] | 7 | $420.00 | Operational | Panasonic | HC-V700MP-K | [illegible] | | |
| 56 | HC-V700M HD Video Camera | 14 | [illegible] | 7 | $420.00 | Operational | Panasonic | HC-V700MP-K | | | |
| 57 | HC-V700M HD Video Camera | 15 | [illegible] | 7 | $420.00 | Operational | Panasonic | HC-V700MP-K | | | |
| 58 | HC-V700M HD Video Camera | 16 | [illegible] | 7 | $420.00 | Operational | Panasonic | HC-V700MP-K | | | |
| 59 | HC-V700M HD Video Camera | 17 | [illegible] | 7 | $420.00 | Operational | Panasonic | HC-V700MP-K | [illegible] | | |
| 60 | HC-V700M HD Video Camera | 18 | [illegible] | 7 | $420.00 | Operational | Panasonic | HC-V700MP-K | [illegible] | | |
| 61 | HC-V700M HD Video Camera | 19 | [illegible] | 7 | $420.00 | Operational | Panasonic | HC-V700MP-K | | | |
| 62 | HC-V700M HD Video Camera | 20 | [illegible] | 7 | $420.00 | Operational | Panasonic | HC-V700MP-K | | | |
| 63 | HC-V700M HD Video Camera | 21 | [illegible] | 7 | $550.00 | Operational | Panasonic | HC-V700MP-K | [illegible] | | [illegible] |
| 64 | HC-V700M HD Video Camera | 22 | [illegible] | 7 | $550.00 | Operational | Panasonic | HC-V700MP-K | [illegible] | | [illegible] |
| 65 | HC-V700M HD Video Camera | 23 | [illegible] | 7 | $550.00 | Operational | Panasonic | HC-V700MP-K | [illegible] | | [illegible] |
| 66 | HC-V700M HD Video Camera | 24 | [illegible] | 7 | $550.00 | Operational | Panasonic | HC-V700MP-K | [illegible] | | [illegible] |
| 67 | HC-V700M HD Video Camera | 25 | [illegible] | 8 | $550.00 | Operational | Panasonic | HC-V700MP-K | [illegible] | | |

**Figure 6.3.** Screenshot of Panasonic HC-V700M Inventory Page

## Labeling the Pieces

Each piece that circulates with the item should be labeled with its name and function. This is most helpful for items that leave the library but could also be done for items that stay in the library because the main purpose is to provide patrons with information about the equipment when they are not near library staff to ask questions. This is also important during checkout for staff members who may not be familiar with all the pieces and are checking out the item to the patron. See figure 6.4 for an example of pieces that are labeled to circulate with an item.

### TEXTBOX 6.1

The term "item" refers to the whole item in the package. The term "main item" refers to the main item that is circulated (e.g., the camera). The term "piece" (or "pieces") refers to the individual things within the item (e.g., battery, SD card, battery charger, and USB cable).

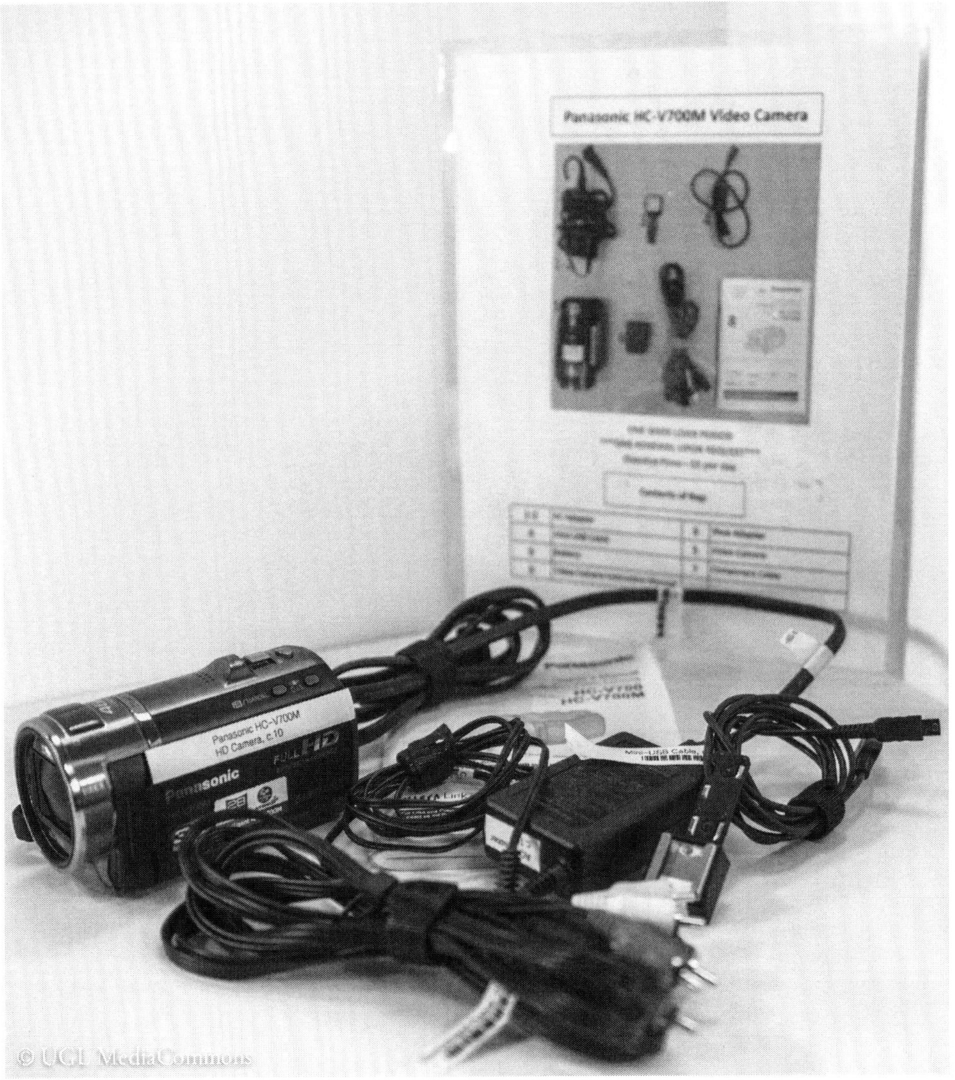


**Figure 6.4.** Picture of Pieces Labeled for an Item

## Creating a Contents Sheet

A contents sheet is a piece of paper that indicates which pieces are included in an item when it circulates. The contents sheet should, at the very least, have a list of all the pieces, but it is best to include a picture of each piece in case the staff member or patron is unfamiliar with what a piece looks like.

Circulating a contents sheet with the item assists with the checkout process and helps the patron make sure all the pieces are in place before returning the item (further discussed in chapter 8). Take a picture of all the pieces laid out (possibly on a sheet of paper as a background). The picture should be zoomed in as close as possible while still displaying all the pieces in focus on a neutral background. Insert the picture into a word-processing or graphic-design program and label each piece numerically. Below that, create a table in which each piece is identified according to the number assigned in the picture. Laminating the contents sheet is recommended for greater durability. Figure 6.5 is an example of a contents sheet.

**Panasonic HC-V700M Video Camera**

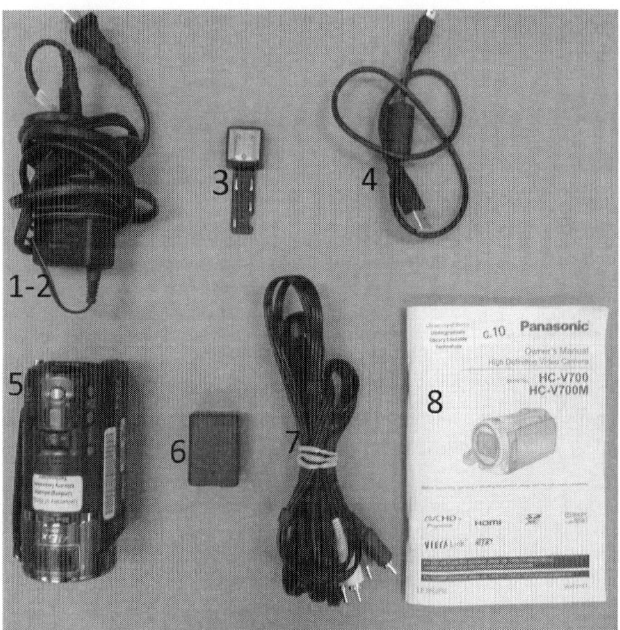


**ONE WEEK LOAN PERIOD**

*****ONE RENEWAL UPON REQUEST*****

**Overdue Fines—$5 per day**

**Contents of Bag:**

| 1-2 | AC Adapter | 3 | Shoe Adapter |
|---|---|---|---|
| 4 | Mini-USB Cable | 5 | Video Camera |
| 6 | Battery | 7 | Component Cable |
| 8 | Video Camera Instruction Manual | | |

**Figure 6.5.** Contents Sheet

A contents sheet could be developed in any word-processing program with which the library staff member is familiar. Depending on the number of pieces included and the size of the package for circulating that item, the contents sheet may be a half or full sheet.

## Equipment-Loan Form

Some libraries may require patrons to sign a loan agreement during the checkout process. The type of form you use will have direct implications for the circulation procedure. Here are some different ways libraries use equipment-loan forms:

**Generic template.** A basic template, with empty fields, that states standard terms and liability of loan. The fields must be filled out each time an equipment item circulates. During checkout, a staff person writes, types, or scans in item-specific information before the patron signs the agreement. An advantage of this form is that there is only one—whenever you want to edit, all you have to do is change it in one place.

**Item-specific form.** Created from the basic template, it is prepopulated with information specific to the item being lent—e.g., a list of all the pieces, the replacement cost, the title. There is one form for every individual item that you lend, and each time an item circulates, a form must be filled out. While having separate forms for each item allows for a speedier checkout process, editing can be time-consuming because you will have to edit each form individually.

**Generic one-time form.** A form that has general lending terms and conditions. When filled out and signed, it covers each equipment checkout over a specified period of time. This form is kept in the filing cabinet discussed in chapter 4 for the predetermined time (e.g., six months, a semester, an academic year).

If you will require patrons to formally agree to the lending terms, discuss with your colleagues the positives and negatives of each form and how using each form will affect your library's circulation procedures. Textbox 6.2 lists some suggested fields for form templates.

In addition to including some or all of the fields suggested, the form should also include spaces for patrons to initial, both upon checkout of the item and upon return of the item. Having patrons initial at different places throughout the equipment-loan agreement

### TEXTBOX 6.2

### SUGGESTED FIELDS FOR TEMPLATES

- Library name/information
- Statistical question (if you keep statistics on how your equipment is used)
- Patron name and library ID
- Checkout date/time
- Return date/time
- Item name, copy number, and barcode
- Pieces included (should be in the same numbered sequence as on the contents sheet)
- Statement of liability
- Terms of loan
- Replacement value

UNIVERSITY OF ILLINOIS AT URBANA – CHAMPAIGN: UNDERGRADUATE LIBRARY

**EQUIPMENT LOAN AGREEMENT**

Please indicate if this is being used for a class project: ___ Yes ___ No. If so, which class: ______________

| FULL PATRON NAME: | | | Library Barcode: | | |
|---|---|---|---|---|---|
| Check out date/ time: | | | Return due date: | | |
| Item: | c. | | Item Barcode: | | |
| *Contents of bag:* ☐ *Pieces* | Patron initials | Staff initials | | Patron initials | Staff initials |
| 1) | 1. | 1. | 5) | 5. | 5. |
| 2) | 2. | 2. | 6) | 6. | 6. |
| 3) | 3. | 3. | 7) | 7. | 7. |
| 4) | 4. | 4. | 8) | 8. | 8. |

New Due Date:______ Staff Initial:______

***Terms of Loan and statement of liability***

*I acknowledge that the replacement value of this item is placed at $ ___ **Borrower Initial**

*I agree to be responsible for replacing any and all parts that are not returned. ___ **Borrower Initial**

*Liability assessment, if any, will be based on "Section 12.1 – Custodianship of Property" in Business and Financial Policies and Procedures. The borrower will be held responsible for replacement of hardware or parts thereof damaged or lost during the loan period. Contact uglcirc@library.uiuc.edu for replacement options.*

*I understand that the library is not responsible for any damage that may occur on equipment as a result of media borrowed from the library. ___ **Borrower Initial**

*I understand that this item **cannot be returned via a book drop box** and that, upon return, the lower portion of this contract must be signed and initialed by the borrower and discharged by a UGL staff member at the UGL Technology Desk. ___ **Borrower Initial**

This item is eligible for one renewal upon request by the borrower. Renewal is subject to item availability and discretion of UGL staff member. Overdue fines of $5/day begin accruing immediately after 9PM on the due date.

By initialing above and signing below, I acknowledge that I have read and accepted the terms of loan and statement of liability above.

Borrower Signature date Staff Name (Print) date

------------------------------------------------------------

***Equipment Return***

The equipment described in this document has been returned to the Undergraduate Library. The equipment will not be discharged until all items are inspected and accounted for by the staff member, and checked off the list by both the patron and the staff member. If a piece in the bag is missing or damaged, the bag will not be discharged from the patron's account.

| Item: *Contents of bag:* ☐ *Pieces* | Patron initials | Staff initials | | Patron initials | Staff initials |
|---|---|---|---|---|---|
| 1) | 1. | 1. | 5) | 5. | 5. |
| 2) | 2. | 2. | 6) | 6. | 6. |
| 3) | 3. | 3. | 7) | 7. | 7. |
| 4) | 4. | 4. | 8) | 8. | 8. |

Received by UGL Staff Member (Print) date Signature of borrower (upon returning) date

Authorization for temporary off-campus use of equipment owned and maintained by the University of Illinois at Urbana – Champaign: Undergraduate Library

Contact: (217) 333-3477 Email: undergrad@library.uiuc.edu

**Figure 6.6.** Equipment-Loan Form Template

draws their attention to specific responsibilities they are agreeing to and gives the library staff an opportunity to go through the terms of agreement in detail. An example of an equipment-loan agreement form is provided in figure 6.6. Figure 6.7 is an example of an equipment-loan agreement form from the Undergraduate Library at the University of Illinois at Urbana-Champaign (UIUC) for one type of camera. Here are more examples of equipment-loan agreement forms from different types of libraries:

- Forbush High School Media Center, Equipment Use Waiver Form for Students: http://www.yadkin.k12.nc.us/webpages/mcarter/files/studentequipmentform updated.pdf

UNIVERSITY OF ILLINOIS AT URBANA – CHAMPAIGN: UNDERGRADUATE LIBRARY

**EQUIPMENT LOAN AGREEMENT**

Please indicate if this is being used for a class project: ___ Yes ___ No. If so, which class: ______________

| FULL PATRON NAME: | | | Library Barcode: | | |
|---|---|---|---|---|---|
| Check out date/ time: | | | Return due date: | | |
| Item: **Panasonic HC-V700M Video Camera** | c. | | Item Barcode: | | |
| *Contents of bag:* 8 *Pieces* | Patron initials | Staff initials | | Patron initials | Staff initials |
| 1/2) AC Adapter (2 pieces) | 1/2. | 1/2. | 6) Battery | 6. | 6. |
| 3) Shoe Adapter | 3. | 3. | 7) Video Camera Instruction Manual | 7. | 7. |
| 4) Mini-USB Cable | 4. | 4. | 8) Component Cable | 8. | 8. |
| 5) Video Camera | 5. | 5. | | | |

New Due Date: ______ Staff Initial: ______

***Terms of Loan and statement of liability***

*I acknowledge that the replacement value of this item is placed at $ 840 ___Borrower Initial

*I agree to be responsible for replacing any and all parts that are not returned. ___Borrower Initial

*Liability assessment, if any, will be based on "Section 12.1 – Custodianship of Property" in Business and Financial Policies and Procedures. The borrower will be held responsible for replacement of hardware or parts thereof damaged or lost during the loan period. Contact uglcirc@library.uiuc.edu for replacement options.*

*I understand that the library is not responsible for any damage that may occur on equipment as a result of media borrowed from the library. ___Borrower Initial

*I understand that this item **cannot be returned via a book drop box** and that, upon return, the lower portion of this contract must be signed and initialed by the borrower and discharged by a UGL staff member at the UGL Technology Desk. ___Borrower Initial

This item is eligible for one renewal upon request by the borrower. Renewal is subject to item availability and discretion of UGL staff member. Overdue fines of $5/day begin accruing immediately after 9PM on the due date.

By initialing above and signing below, I acknowledge that I have read and accepted the terms of loan and statement of liability above.

Borrower Signature date Staff Name (Print) date

---

## *Equipment Return*

The equipment described in this document has been returned to the Undergraduate Library. The equipment will not be discharged until all items are inspected and accounted for by the staff member, and checked off the list by both the patron and the staff member. If a piece in the bag is missing or damaged, the bag will not be discharged from the patron's account.

| *Contents of bag:* 8 *Pieces* | Patron initials | Staff initials | | Patron initials | Staff initials |
|---|---|---|---|---|---|
| 1/2) AC Adapter (2 pieces) | 1/2. | 1/2. | 6) Battery | 6. | 6. |
| 3) Shoe Adapter | 3. | 3. | 7) Video Camera Instruction Manual | 7. | 7. |
| 4) Mini-USB Cable | 4. | 4. | 8) Component Cable | 8. | 8. |
| 5) Video Camera | 5. | 5. | | | |

Received by UGL Staff Member (Print) date Signature of borrower (upon returning) date

Authorization for temporary off-campus use of equipment owned and maintained by the University of Illinois at Urbana – Champaign: Undergraduate Library
Contact: (217) 333-3477 Email: undergrad@library.uiuc.edu

**Figure 6.7.** Panasonic HC-V700M HD Camera Equipment-Loan Form

- Hornell City School District, Agreement for School Digital Equipment Loan Use: http://www.toolboxpro.org/secure/teachers/2703/130904013400_Digital_Equipment_Use_form.docx
- MIT Lewis Music Library, iPad Computer Liability Agreement: http://libraries.mit.edu/wp-content/uploads/2013/04/iPad_liability_agreement_9132.pdf
- University of Arizona Library, Equipment Loan Agreement: http://www.library.arizona.edu/sites/default/files/users/djbuffin/Laptop-and-Projector-Agreement-July-2013.pdf
- University of Maryland Libraries, Borrowers Registration and Liability Agreement: https://libumd.wufoo.com/forms/borrowers-registration-liability-agreement/

- University of Pennsylvania Weigle Information Commons, Equipment Lending Program Guidelines: http://wic.library.upenn.edu/multimedia/docs/eqloanguide.pdf
- Wellesley High School Library, Student Equipment Loan Form, 2013–2014: http://www.wellesley.k12.ma.us/sites/wellesleyps/files/file/file/studentequipmentloanform_0.pdf

Many libraries do not require an equipment-loan agreement form to be filled out upon checkout. A good reason for requiring this practice, however, is that the agreement notifies the patron of specific terms and liabilities involved in borrowing equipment and helps the billing department keep patrons accountable.

## Web Page

Once new equipment is cataloged and processed, it will be important to update the loanable technology program's web page with information about the item. The web page should have a list of technology that is available, as well as a link to the catalog record so that the patron will receive real-time information about how many copies of the item are available. The web page is helpful because it can provide more information about specific models than the catalog record. It can include links to training documentation, videos, or internally developed information sheets. Figure 6.8 is an example of what a loanable

**Figure 6.8.** Screenshot of Loanable Technology Website

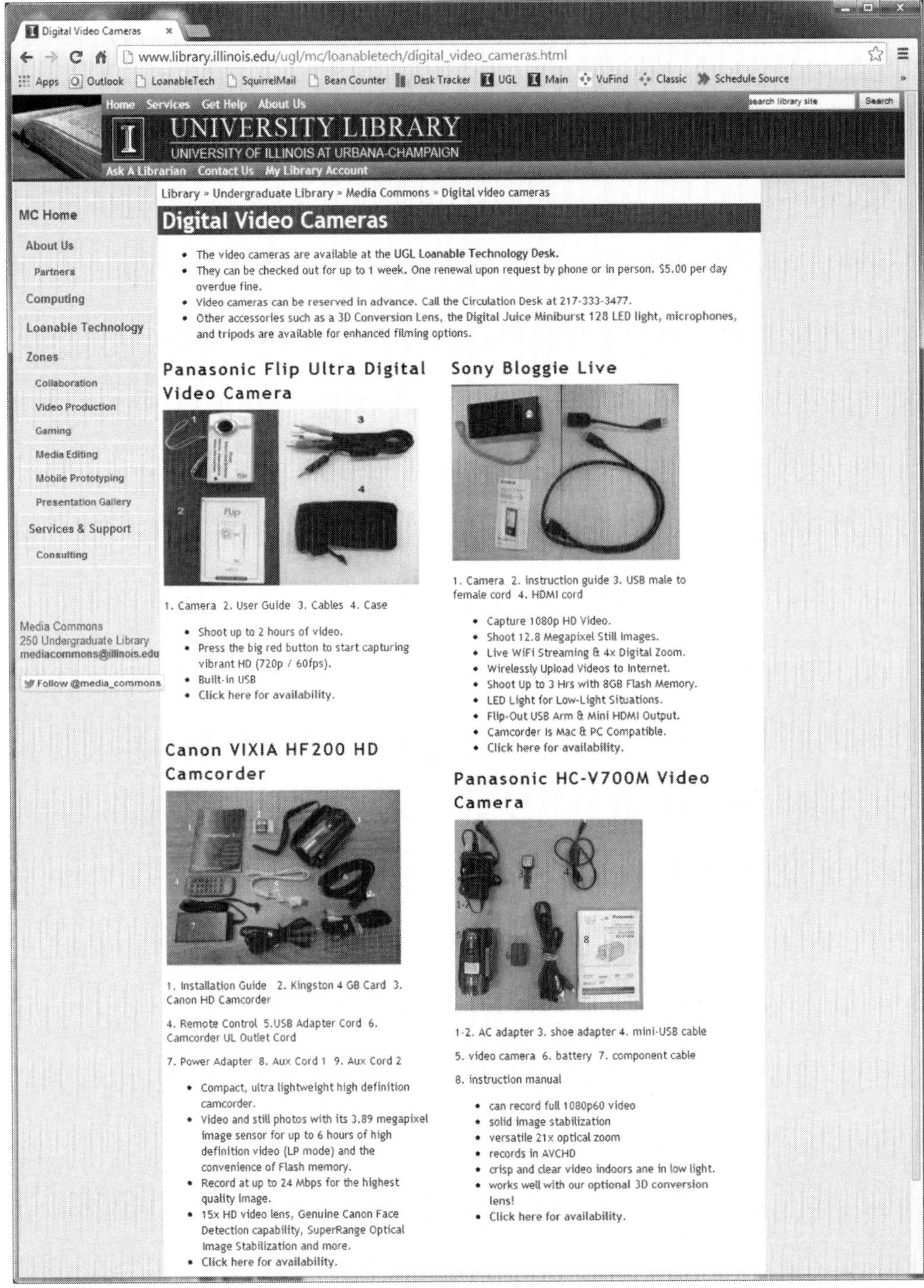


**Figure 6.9.** Screenshot of Website for Video Cameras

technology home page could look like, while figure 6.9 is an example of a website that is specific to a type of item. Here are other examples of loanable technology web pages:

- Albuquerque Public Schools: http://www.aps.edu/professional-learning/instructional-learning-technologies/multimedia-resources
- Brooklyn Public Library: http://www.bklynpubliclibrary.org/only-bpl/tablet-lending-program
- University of Arizona: http://www.library.arizona.edu/services/equipment-lending

- University of Nebraska–Lincoln: http://libraries.unl.edu/DigitalMediaEquipment
- Williams College: http://oit.williams.edu/equip-loan/

Organizing web pages by equipment categories can also help patrons who know what kind of equipment they want but do not know what options are available. For examples, see http://www.library.illinois.edu/ugl/mc/loanable.html (UIUC Undergraduate Library) and http://wic.library.upenn.edu/wicfacilities/lending.html (University of Pennsylvania Weigle Information Commons). This type of organization helps patrons make informed decisions before they approach the desk to inquire about checking out the item, or in the case of the Weigle Information Commons, before they reserve the item online.

## Packaging Items

Selecting the right package for circulation of an item is important for many reasons. Some items will be fine if they circulate in a plastic or vinyl bag, while other items will be better protected by a bag with more padding. Some items may not need packaging at all—just a label on the side might be appropriate. Additionally, libraries serve different populations; what works for an item at a school library, for example, may be very different from what works for the same item at a public library. Ask the following questions when evaluating which packaging to purchase:

**Is a package needed?** If it is a single item, perhaps an identification tag can be adhered directly to the item. Evaluate the durability of the item to determine if it might be better protected in some package. If there is more than one piece, it is best to include them all together in some package.

**What size package is needed?** Measure the item to be packaged and then add at least one inch in height, width, and depth to make room for package thickness and accompanying pieces.

**Will the item fit on shelves or in the cabinet once it is packaged?** For example, if multiple items will be included in a backpack it will be important to find a backpack that will fit in the designated space. If not, will the packaging protect the item in an open area?

**Is the packaging durable and is the brand reputable?** Read user reviews. Look for reviews written by people who have used or owned the package for a while to see if it holds up under heavy use.

**What color do you want?** Are there a lot of dark-colored pieces that will circulate with the item? If so, you might want a bag with a lighter interior. Are you planning to purchase all the same exterior color for uniformity? Or do you want different-colored bags that serve as visual cues for the equipment they contain?

**Does the package need to have handles or straps?** An item may be small enough that it can be put in a bag or backpack and does not need handles. Bags with handles offer options for carrying the item, which may be safer than just putting it on top of other books or materials, which could allow it to slip off and fall to the floor.

**Do you prefer a zipper, Velcro, or another way of closing the bag?** Which option is best for the item? Some of this may depend on the weight and size of the item.

**Is the cost within your price range?** Are there alternate options for packaging or is the selected product worth the added cost because of some feature that is needed for the equipment? Also remember to include tax and shipping (if applicable) in the total purchase cost.

Plastic cash-handling bags work well for cords, adapters, and more durable items (like external hard drives), and different-sized and -colored padded bags for all the other equipment. Some equipment, like projectors or tripods, comes with a bag that is specifically meant for housing that item as well as all the cords and accessories that come with it. It is most convenient if the package comes with the equipment (even if that means paying a little extra) because the distinctive bag means easier identification when staff and students are locating the equipment in the cabinets. For items that do not come with packaging, like external DVD drives, it may be best to choose packaging that makes them visually distinctive. Figure 6.10 provides some examples of packaging.

**TEXTBOX 6.3**

Recommendation: Purchase at least one extra of every package or bag you intend to use. This sets you up for quick turnaround time if you need to replace a bag for some reason or purchase a new copy of the item that the package houses. This is also a good idea in case the package is discontinued before you need to order more.

**Figure 6.10.** Examples of Packaging

## Labeling the Outside of the Package

Labeling the exterior of the package with identifying information is key to helping staff members efficiently serve your patrons. Two options for this are generating labels from a label machine or using luggage tags (figure 6.11), although a laminated tag would work as well. The labeling should be informative but not too busy with text—you may think about including a QR code that will lead the patron directly to the lending-policies page. Suggestions of what to include on the tag or label include:

- name of item and copy number of the item
- barcode
- library contact information
- circulation period (e.g., two-hour in-library use, or one-week loan)
- renewal policy
- overdue fine amounts (if your library charges fines)
- return instructions (if there are special policies on returns)

Figure 6.11 is an example of the luggage tags that UIUC uses. This tag was chosen because of its size and durability. The hard plastic does not wear out (or at least it has not in the six years that UIUC has been using them), and the surface area is just large enough to fit a barcode, the title of the item, and the copy number on one side, and a couple of stickers on the back. Figure 6.12 shows the tag after it has been stickered for circulation.

Occasionally a zip tie is needed to connect the tag to the item's package, but most of the time the original band can be used. This kind of luggage tag comes in several colors as well. Using different colors helps to distinguish between item models. For instance, UIUC's circulating iPad 2s have black tags, but the iPad 3s have yellow. Another example is that UIUC's flash drives that leave the library have yellow tags, but the flash drives that stay in the library have green tags.

**TEXTBOX 6.4**

Recommendation: Do an Amazon.com search for any labeling or packaging supplies—there is a vast variety there and Amazon's product suggestions may help even further. Do a comparison with other vendors as well. Your business department may need to purchase items from a particular vendor, but at least do the initial search for best value and item.

**Figure 6.11.** Picture of Travelon Luggage Tag without Stickers

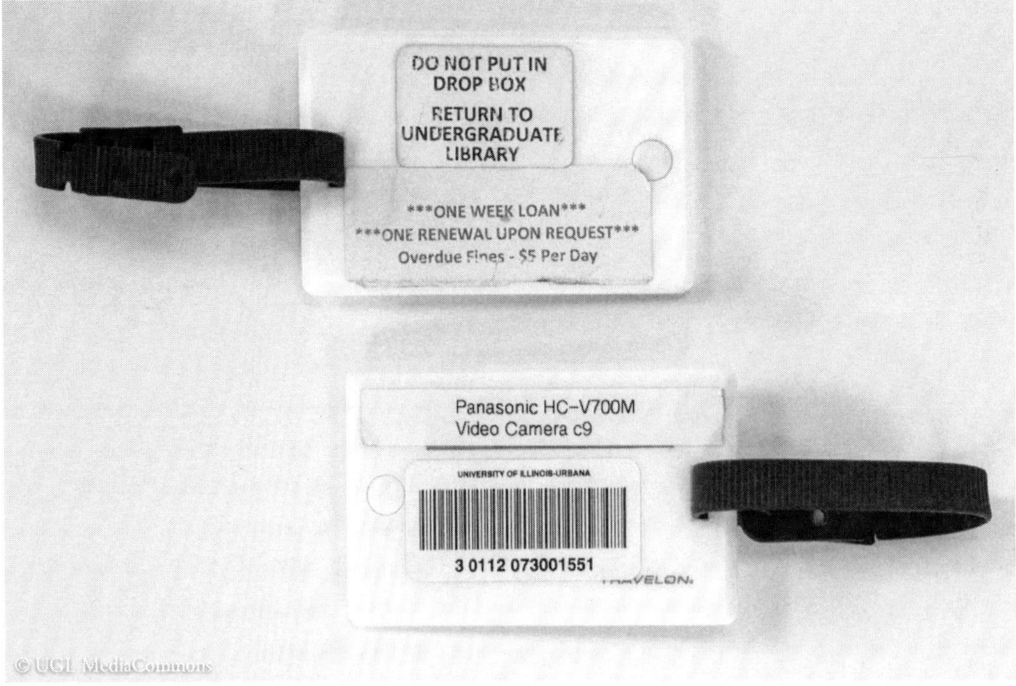

**Figure 6.12.** Front and Back of Luggage Tag with Stickers and Barcode

## Labeling the Main Item

After the equipment is cataloged, packaged, and labeled, there are a few additional steps to complete before a patron can check it out. Label the main piece of equipment that circulates. An example of a "main item" is a camera or a handheld gaming device or a projector (which may have accessories that should be packaged with it, like SD cards, cables, cords, or remote controls). A patron who picks up the item for the first time may need assistance discovering where the power cord plugs in or where the SD card slot is. Pointing these things out will enhance usability after the patron has left the point of service. The following list is not exhaustive, but it should give you an idea of the things that you may want to label:

- any ports that may not be obvious: USB, HDMI, VGA
- power button
- how to open the item (e.g., a button or something to slide)
- battery compartment
- button to turn on the device's WiFi (Wireless Internet Access)
- SD card slot

What you label will depend on the item and the population to which you are catering. The less expensive and usually less complex items might circulate to patrons who

**TEXTBOX 6.5**

"Main item" refers to the main piece of equipment that circulates. An example would be a camera or a projector or a handheld gaming device.

are less familiar with technology and who may need a little more assistance locating the main features. The more expensive items, which are usually the more complex items, will probably cater to a patron group that already knows basic operating features, but even so, good labeling and a guide with quick tips could be useful.

In addition to labeling key parts of the main item, it is also a good idea to label the item in a prominent place with the barcode itself and other library identification. At UIUC, Panasonic camcorders are labeled with where to plug in the AC adapter, the barcode, the name of the item and copy number, and Undergraduate Library identification. The AC adapter plug is labeled because the placement is not obvious on the camera and may be difficult for the user to locate. All the other labels are for identification only.

Label everything that might not be immediately obvious to the user. Place yourself in the shoes of a patron using the item for the first time. Imagine what a patron would think if they have never used this equipment before, and use those questions as a reference for deciding what to label. Be aware of your internal dialogue and pretend that the patron is thinking through those same things. Where is the power button? Where is the battery? Is the battery charged? Where is the storage? How do I press play? How do I get the screen to turn on? What do I need to open to plug in my adapter or cable for uploading and downloading information? Use the questions as a guide for labeling. Figure 6.13 is an example of a main item (Panasonic camera) that has been labeled.

**Figure 6.13.** Example of Labels for the Panasonic Camera

## Labeling the Individual Pieces

Before all the pieces are placed in the package, determine if each piece should be labeled so that it is obvious that they are all part of the same set. In this case, each piece should be labeled with the copy number of the main item (e.g., camcorder copy 4 would have all the items in that package labeled with camcorder copy 4) and possibly the barcode so that the piece can be matched with the item easily. This method then allows for pieces to be returned easily to the correct package. For example, if a group of four students each checks out a camcorder package and they all use their camcorders at the same time and in the same place, they can easily sort the items so that copy 2 pieces do not end up in copy 4's bag. This also makes it easier for the circulation staff to check the pieces (and sort them, if needed) when the item is checked in.

Another way to circulate the pieces is to have only the main piece labeled and then have a box full of accessories (e.g., cords, adapters, chargers, batteries) that the staff person adds to the bag upon checkout. Or those accessories could each be labeled separately. For instance, if a patron wants to check out an iPad, the iPad is in its labeled bag. When the patron checks it out, the staff person gets an AC adapter and a charging cable from a box and includes them in the bag. Or the staff person gets the additional pieces and checks them out too. A drawback of this is that once the main item is returned and checked in, there is no way to confirm who checked out the auxiliary parts if they turn out to be broken or missing. In this scenario, the staff person has to be extremely vigilant to check each item as it is being returned, with the patron present, to verify that everything has been returned in good order. If each part is separately cataloged, labeled, and checked out, it is on the patron's record. Another drawback when the auxiliary items are not automatically included with the main item is that either the staff person or the patron needs to know which other items to check out with that main item.

There may be instances to use both of these methods, but whichever method or combination of methods is used, make sure that the staff is trained in how to check out the items so that the patron leaves with all the needed pieces.

At times creativity may be needed for finding solutions to packaging and labeling. For example, UIUC discovered that patrons were checking out (often brand new) MacBook chargers and swapping them with their own broken or frayed ones before returning them. The patrons would also switch the labels and barcode stickers to the broken charger so that when the circulation staff checked it in, they would see that the barcode matched and then check it in. Many times, the circulation staff might not be alerted to the problem until the next patron checked it out and discovered it was not working. The loanable technology desk manager tried many deterrents, like etching the letters "UGL" (Undergraduate Library) on the square AC adapter, but in a few cases patrons scratched "UGL" on their broken one before turning it back in. For a while, UIUC also tried drawing a purple ring around each of the ends near the plugs, but that was too subtle and it often wore off quickly.

Finally, it was decided that there needed to be something more visible, which is when colored duct tape was suggested. UIUC now hides two strips of tattle tape under a wrap of duct tape on the square part of the charger and also puts pieces of duct tape near the ends of the cords. The chargers are still labeled with barcodes and copy numbers, but that is on top of the duct tape. Since this has been done to all the MacBook chargers, there have not been any further instances of theft of this item (see figure 6.14). The colored duct tape has been so successful that now a different color is used for each of the different types of chargers that are lent out (45W, 60W, and 85W), both for security purposes and because the colored tape serves as a visual cue that assists staff and student assistants when they are looking for chargers in the cabinet. This is an instance of how extreme measures in labeling have been beneficial for the loanable technology program.

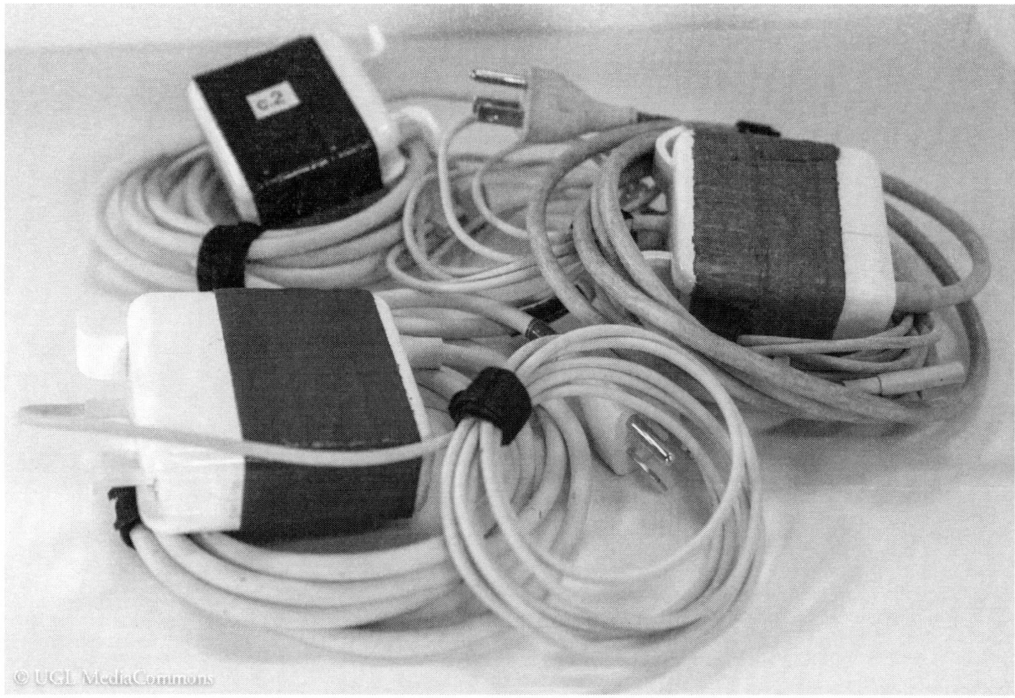


**Figure 6.14.** MacBook Pro Charger, MacBook Pro 85W, MacBook Air 45W Chargers

**TEXTBOX 6.6**

Label each piece that circulates in the package with, at the very least, the library name. The more information available on the label, the better—this is especially helpful in tracking an item if it is stolen or misplaced.

# Housing Items

Chapter 4 discussed how to determine which cabinets to purchase, but this section will discuss organizing and labeling the cabinets that have been purchased and put in place.

## Organizing Items in Cabinets

The following questions may help guide the organization of shelves and cabinets.

- Which items will be used most frequently? Put those items closest to the circulation point.
- Are there items that are not allowed to leave the library? Think about putting all of them together on one shelf or in one cabinet, along with good signage as a reminder that these are in-library use only items.
- Do more expensive items need to be kept in a more secure location or a locked cabinet?
- Are the shelves moveable to accommodate larger or smaller items? If so, plan for the larger items to be organized together in those areas. Leave room on the shelf to allow for growth if there are plans to acquire more items.

**TEXTBOX 6.7**

Separating the items for in-library use and out-of-library use into their own cabinets cuts down on confusion for your staff.

Cabinets may need to be rearranged periodically, especially when new loanable technology items are added to the collection. In this way the loanable technology collection is somewhat like the book collection—when new books are added, sometimes the stacks need to be shifted in order to accommodate new items.

## Labeling the Exterior of Cabinets

Labeling the exterior of the loanable technology cabinets is a strategy that helps students and staff quickly locate items. Perhaps your library already has a way of labeling doors to indicate what is inside. If not, then this is a good opportunity to develop a template for that purpose. Regardless of the program used to create the template, use images and the largest font possible. Having well-labeled cabinets will help with item retrieval and service efficiency.

The placement of the items in the cabinet should be mirrored in the sign on the exterior of the cabinet. For example, if the cabinet has four shelves, there should be four lines on the sign. Likewise, images should be placed on each line (shelf) where they would be in the cabinet. These subtle reminders serve as subconscious finding aids that help staff and students locate the item that is going to be checked out. Use as many pictures as possible to supplement the text on the sign. Having a visual representation of the item as part of the retrieval process will help reinforce staff and student-assistant knowledge about the loanable technology collection. The images also remind them what the item should look like when they get it out of the bag or if they glance at the cabinet to see if the item is available without looking it up in the catalog.

Figure 6.15 is an example of an exterior cabinet-door sign, and figure 6.16 demonstrates how the placement of the items on the sign mirrors the placement of the items in the cabinet.

Use the catalog name of the items for every label. For example, if the catalog name is "Lumix ZR1 Digital Camera," that should be the phrase that is used on the exterior sign. The student or staff will remember the catalog name as they move from the computer to the cabinet. This reduces slang or shortened versions of the names, which, in turn, decreases communication errors by reinforcing the exact brand, make, and model of the technology.

## Labeling the Interior of Cabinets

Providing as many visual cues as possible does aid with item retrieval, and one of those visual cues is labeling the actual shelves inside the cabinets. Shelf labeling could include another picture of the item that was used on the outside of the cabinet, but it could also be a text label that gives the name and number of items that should be there. In a cabinet that includes many similar things, such as different types of calculators, labeling

**Loanable Technology Cabinet #4**

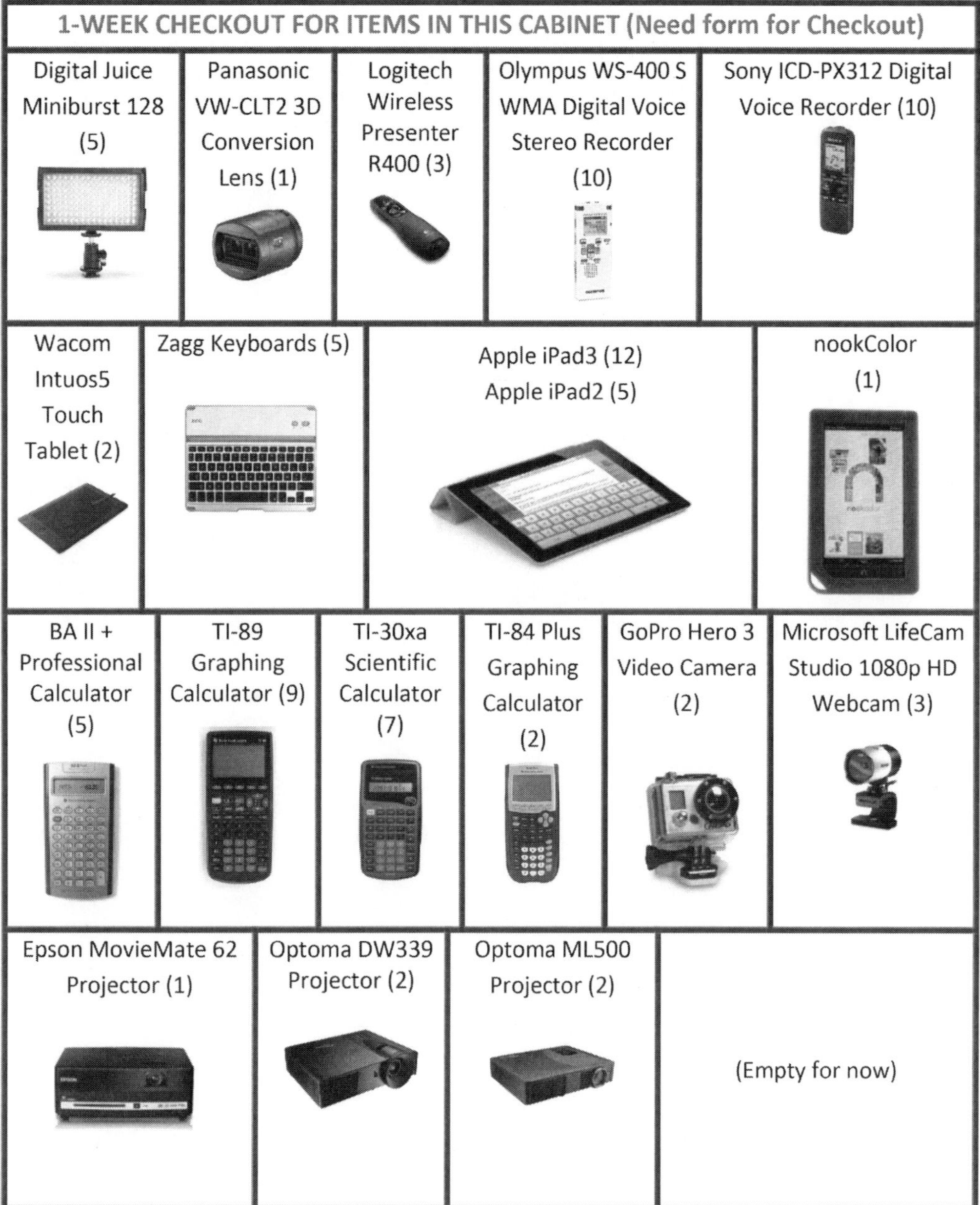


**Figure 6.15.** Loanable Technology Cabinet-Door Sign

also identifies where the items should be placed upon return. The more labeling that is done, the better prepared the staff will be for service. Use a label machine to create and print labels for the shelves inside the cabinets. The labels can be easily removed and replaced when they need to be updated. Use the name of the item and the number of copies available for checkout so that students and staff can plan for appropriate space when putting the items back after they are returned. Figure 6.17 is an example of interior cabinet labeling.

**Figure 6.16.** Interior of Loanable Technology Cabinet

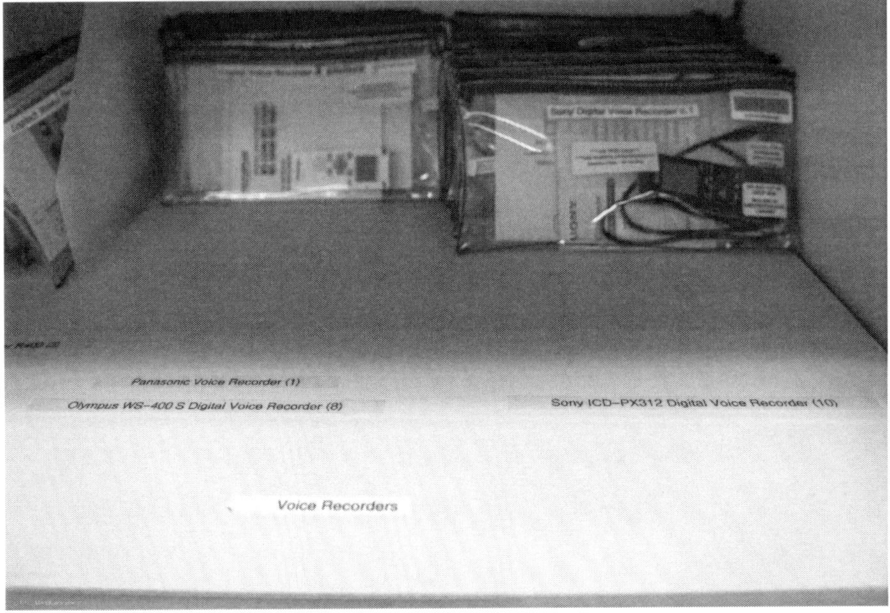


**Figure 6.17.** Image of a Shelf with Multiple Labels

**TEXTBOX 6.8**

Use the exact name of the item as it appears in the catalog. Consistency in names is key, especially as your loanable technology collection expands.

## Key Points

This chapter has discussed some simple yet practical ways to prepare loanable equipment for circulation. Some of the main recommendations are below.

- Purchase at least one extra of every package or bag you intend to use.
- Label everything you think is not immediately obvious to the user. In addition to labeling key parts of the item, it is also a good idea to label the item in a prominent place with the barcode itself and other institutional identification.
- Organize cabinets based on usage, item similarity, and loan period. Put similar items together—for instance, all the cameras in one cupboard or on the same shelf. Then, put all the camera accessories nearby, or in the same cabinet as the cameras, so that the staff and student assistants will not have to go far to retrieve multiple items for patrons. Separate items for in-library use and those for out-of-library use into different areas.
- Put a sign on the exterior of the cabinets with images of the items inside (using a large font to label the items). The sign should mirror the contents of the cabinet.
- Consistent naming is another way to reinforce item brand, make, and model for your staff and student employees. Make sure to clearly label the interior shelves (with terms identical to those used on the exterior sign) and use images as well to help when items are returned.

Packaging, labeling, and intuitively planning how to house loanable technology are essential parts of setting up your staff and students for efficient customer service. The next chapter will provide some policies to consider for your program.

CHAPTER 7

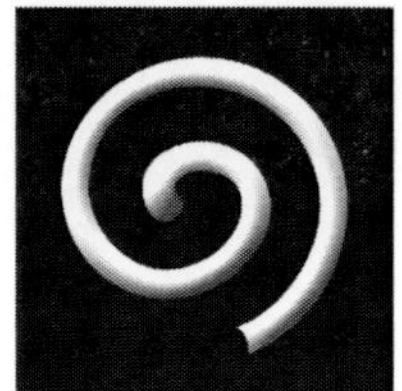

# Creating Policies

**IN THIS CHAPTER**

- ▷ Collection development for loanable technology, including statement for donated and gift items
- ▷ Academic versus personal use of an item
- ▷ Borrowing privileges
- ▷ Loan periods
- ▷ Renewals
- ▷ Reservation of items
- ▷ Lost, stolen, or unreturned items
- ▷ Privacy and confidentiality

SEVERAL ASPECTS OF loanable technology warrant policies that might differ from circulation policies for other library materials. In addition to a collection development policy, other statements or policies should be developed to cover borrowing privileges, checkout periods, renewals, reserved items, and lost, stolen, or unreturned items. It is also important to determine policies for academic versus personal use of an item. These statements and policies should be included on the library's loanable technology web page, as well as any policy web pages, so all patrons can view them and staff can refer to them when explaining expectations and procedures. Because a staff person cannot communicate every policy to a patron who requests an item, it is important to at least have the policies available so that staff can refer to them and patrons can review them. This chapter covers the policies needed to manage a loanable technology program. Examples of several policies are included in textbox 7.5 at the end of this chapter.

## Collection Development Policy

As previously discussed, the library needs to determine the type of equipment to purchase, including how many of each item and when to replace the item. Frequent assessment of need and use of items is critical in order to understand if the program is providing the support for its mission. These topics were discussed in chapter 2. Your collection development policy should include the intent of the collection, target audience, scope of the collection, selection procedure, potential target number of items to maintain, procedures for donations, and collection maintenance. It should also include if there are categories within the collection, such as items for in-library use only or items that can circulate outside the library.

Commonly requested technology generally falls into one of two categories: items that would make a user's stay in a library more convenient, and items that are too expensive for the average person to purchase. Usually, items requested in the first category are items that would typically stay in the library (chargers, USB cables, headphones, etc.), and items in the second category are those that would be allowed to leave the library (cameras, voice recorders, speakers, projectors, handheld gaming equipment, etc.).

Even if not communicated on a website to patrons, the library should have guidelines for the maximum number of laptops, cameras, tablets, voice recorders, or other technology to have and if they are available only in-house or allowed to circulate outside the library. It is likely that your library will never be able to have enough items to satisfy the needs of all patrons, so it is useful to establish a cap on purchases. Determinants for items to purchase (and for the number of each item to purchase, as discussed in chapter 3) include:

- compliance with loanable technology mission
- perceived need
- functionality
- practicality
- cost

### Donations of Items

Chapter 3 briefly discussed how item donations can augment a collection. Typically, a collection development policy also discusses gift items. Loanable technology could be treated much the same as any donation to the library. The item would need to be evaluated to determine if it would be a valuable contribution to the library. Even though it may be freely donated, there is still a cost in evaluating the item, determining if it is needed, creating a cataloging record for it, processing it, and creating checkout forms. Any time

**TEXTBOX 7.1**

**TWO EXAMPLES OF GIFT POLICIES**

- St. Edwards University Munday Library: http://library.stedwards.edu/about/policies/gifts-and-donations
- University of Illinois Libraries: http://www.library.illinois.edu/cmservices/gifts_policy.html

an item is donated, the gift policy should be made clear to the donor, especially when the gift policy dictates that if the library decides not to acquire the item, it may not be returned to the donor.

## Academic versus Personal Use

When developing a collection development policy, it will be important to decide if all equipment will be made available to all eligible patrons, or if distinctions will be made based on individual cases. The policy might communicate the intended audience, types of approved use of the equipment, and types of equipment that will be made available.

For example, if highest priority will be given for projects related to class need, that should be stated. Additionally, if there is frequent demand for equipment to create a multimedia presentation, such as a video or audio podcast for class, then part of the equipment collected should support those needs. Communication with those patrons will help you understand if a basic recorder or voice recorder, or even a kit to use with their smartphone, is sufficient. There are instances when the skill of the patron or the quality of output desired necessitates special or higher-end equipment. Some common examples are for recording sports events, recitals, or promotional videos, or for a video camera to attach to a bike helmet. There are many varieties of cameras, tripods, lights, lenses, and accessories that need to be reviewed. A collection development policy is an opportunity to create guidelines for both the types of equipment and the amount that the library will acquire. The mission and collection development policies of the library should include use cases for items, such as if items may be used for extracurricular or recreational needs. One example from the Elmer E. Rasmuson Library at the University of Alaska–Fairbanks states:

> The Rasmuson Library lends media equipment to UAF staff, students, and faculty for **on-campus**, **academic** use. Equipment (such as laptops, digital cameras, digital video recorders and more) is available on a first-come, first-served basis and instructional use takes priority over all other requests. (http://library.uaf.edu/media)

At the Undergraduate Library of the University of Illinois at Urbana-Champaign (UIUC), the intended technology and collection use is included in the overall mission statement of the library.

> The mission of the Undergraduate Library is to provide academic, co-curricular, cultural, and technological support to our users and to be a dynamic, innovative unit. (http://www.library.illinois.edu/ugl/about/vision.html)

and

> The primary focus of the Undergraduate Library (UGL) collection is to serve the research, curriculum, and personal information needs of undergraduate students. (http://www.library.illinois.edu/ugl/about/collection_policy.html)

If policies include specific use examples, it is easier to justify the use of the equipment for various purposes. A useful strategy that helps with collection development and assessment purposes is to ask patrons to indicate on the checkout form if a technology item is being used for a class (and if so, which class) or some extracurricular need. This helps with assessing the program and fulfilling future needs. Every library will need to determine if there should be restrictions on the equipment. It might be difficult to prove if an item is really being checked out for academic or personal use, but if the use policy states that the purpose is to support academic use, then a staff member can emphasize that.

Public libraries may not have the same need to consider how an item is being used as far as academic or recreational need, but their mission statements may also indicate that they provide materials and services to help community residents obtain information that meets their personal, educational, cultural, recreational, and professional needs. Some libraries do restrict some uses of their materials or may charge a fee. For example, as in the case of the Langworthy Public Library in Rhode Island, the mission statement mentions their primary clientele, their services for state residents, and nonresident fees:

> The Langworthy Public Library serves as its primary clientele the people of the Town of Hopkinton and the surrounding communities without regard for age, sex, religious or ethnic background, political affiliation, educational ability or economic status. As a member of the Ocean State Libraries (OSL), the Library further extends full access to it's [*sic*] materials and services at no charge to the people of the state of Rhode Island, as well as to residents of other states who pay a yearly non-resident fee of $115.00. (http://langworthylibrary.org/?page_id=1507)

**TEXTBOX 7.2**

Develop a system to allow patrons to indicate how they are using an item (e.g., to complete a class assignment, to shoot video of a sporting event, or to record an interview). This information will help you understand how the public is using the equipment and will help you with future purchases and training needs.

## Circulation, Borrowing, and Renewal Policies

Of all policies, these are some of the most important. These policies and guidelines need to be established and consistently adhered to by all staff. If not, patrons (and staff) can become frustrated. When establishing a loanable technology program, the temptation may be to just use the existing policy for book and media loans. There are, however, various instances when additional guidelines and decisions need to be made that apply only to loanable technology.

When a book is returned, it is easy to discharge it and return it to the correct shelf. A technology item, though, may require additional steps that will keep the item out of circulation for a day or so before it is ready for recirculation. You may want to check that all pieces have been returned and are functioning or that the internal equipment memory has been wiped of any personal data before the item circulates to another patron.

You will need to establish a process to wipe the memory of each device that stores data before it can circulate again. This includes cameras and other media recording devices, SD cards, USB flash drives, iPads, iPods and other media players, voice recorders, and external hard drives. In some cases there may be an automated process or program for this. Regardless, a standard should be set in place for how quickly this process will occur, whether it is within a few hours of check-in so that the item is ready to circulate or whether there needs to be a buffer period between the time the item is returned and when it will be allowed to circulate again. For libraries that do not have a high circulation rate, it may be possible to take care of an item as soon as it returns. However, if your library has a high demand for the equipment, and few staff to tend to it, you may need to establish a practice to set the equipment aside to be sure that someone is able to carefully finish everything that is needed, such as wiping the device and checking that everything is in proper working condition. Your policy should indicate the chosen practice. At UIUC the written policy is to allow one full day and two overnights between check-in and checkout. If an item is due back to the library at 9:00 p.m. on a Tuesday, it is kept out of circulation a full day before it is able to be reserved or checked out again, making Thursday morning the next time the item can be checked out or reserved. This practice evolved over a period of time, but it allows staff to maintain the functionality of the technology items and also provides a day's buffer in case a patron does not turn in an item on time. In that case, they are notified that the item is due and if a patron is waiting for it. The Fondren Library at Rice University has a similar practice in that they require equipment to be returned by 3:00 p.m. on the third day, since they allow three-day loans for equipment (https://library.rice.edu/services/dmc/about/policies/policies#DMC%20Reservation%20Procedure).

The policy should also include information about how many items a patron can have out at the same time or how many times they can renew an item. For example, a patron may attempt to bypass the system of one-week camera checkout and one renewal by reserving a different copy of the camera every couple of weeks, thus monopolizing a camera for a whole semester. A policy page should explain what is possible and provide reasons for the decisions. The UIUC Undergraduate Library's loanable technology checkout policy provides an example of this.

> The Library is only able to provide a limited number of loanable technology items and the intent is to provide short-term access to these items for class projects and needs. Most loanable technology items can be checked out if there are no other reservations for that item. The Library reserves the right to deny renewal of items in order to best accommodate needs of others who may need the item. **Visit our list of technology for checkout** for more information. Because of the high demand for these items, it is not possible to check out more than one item type (such as only one camera or camcorder—regardless of brand). **The library also requires a 72 hour interval upon the return of an item before a similar item can be checked out.** However, it is appropriate to check out different types of media (e.g. tripod, camera, mic, voice recorder, etc.). Exceptions may be made at the discretion of Library administration. (http://www.library.illinois.edu/ugl/mc/loanable-tech/tech_checkout.html)

### TEXTBOX 7.3

If equipment is not available for immediate checkout after another patron returns it, make sure all staff are able to communicate reasons to a patron (i.e., staff need to check that the equipment is in good working order, that personal information has been erased, and that all paperwork has been correctly processed).

The policy on borrowing and renewing loanable technology should include the following parameters, which will be described below:

- eligibility
- checkout period
- fines and fees
- lost/not returned policy
- renewing technology
- returning technology

**Eligibility.** Who is allowed to check out an item. This policy states whether a patron needs a particular library card or needs to sign some forms to borrow equipment. At academic libraries, it may be that only those affiliated with the institution are allowed to borrow equipment. School libraries might restrict checkout only to teachers who then take responsibility for the item. They may also have forms that require parent signatures. The policy for the Brewbaker Technology Magnet High School Media Center (http://www.brewtech.mps-al.org/?PageName=%27Library%27), for example, indicates that a parent or guardian must sign an equipment-loan permission form that will be kept on file for the current school year. The form also must be signed by a teacher and submitted by 1:00 pm the day equipment is to be checked out.

**Checkout period.** How long an item can circulate. The checkout period for technology can vary from two hours of in-library use to several days or weeks for out-of-library use. It is best to have a standard time period for all technology, such as one day, three days, five days, one week, or two weeks. Often, libraries begin with a shorter time period if they have limited equipment and then with additional purchases may modify it to a longer period, depending on demand.

**Fines and fees.** For overdue, damaged, or lost equipment. The policy should include how much patrons will be charged if the item is late, lost, or damaged. You may want to include all of this on the form that patrons sign when they check out the item. Some libraries might include it in their library catalog record. The same fine structure as for books might be used (nonrecoverable processing fee, for example), but there may be additional fees for the cost of replacing the item. Your policy might also address whether you will allow patrons to replace an item with another of the same brand and model and in a similar condition to the item that was damaged or lost. It is usually preferable to have patrons bring in a replacement item and just charge them the processing fee (much the same as with books) if the item is comparable. Often they might find the item at a cheaper price than what the library might find, and the turnaround time for putting the item into circulation is much less than going through the institutional billing process and then hoping the library will receive those funds. In some libraries, when a patron is billed for an item, the library might never recover that cost directly because the funds may go to a centralized unit to redistribute in the next academic year.

**Lost/not returned policy.** The policy for items that are lost or not returned can be based on the policy in place for books or other items, but it should be adapted for loanable technology. Circulating technology is not the same as circulating books. It is usually more difficult and expensive to replace technology, which is why there should be a shorter amount of time allotted before the patron is billed for a lost item. Your library will need to determine when a technology item is declared lost. A suggestion is for your system to declare a one-week loanable technology item lost after ten days of being overdue. A

**TEXTBOX 7.4**

- Recommendation: Provide the fines and fees policy information on a web page so that any staff member can direct a patron to those policies.

designated staff member should be responsible for letting patrons know if a technology item is overdue and that after ten days they will be charged a replacement cost if the item is not returned. The shorter time period for declaring a loanable technology item lost was needed at the UIUC Undergraduate Library so that patrons actually returned items, rather than keeping them as long as possible for a minimal fee (as with books).

**Renewing technology.** The policy for renewing technology should also include how to renew (in person, over the phone, by voicemail, by e-mail), who can authorize a renewal, and whom to contact for an exception. This is a process that will probably differ from that of books or other materials, for which patrons often request to override a block if the maximum number of renewals has been reached. In the case of equipment, libraries may need to establish a strict policy of not allowing renewals, or allowing only one, because of limited equipment. It is important to establish if patrons can renew items independently through the library catalog or if patrons need to call or come in person to renew items. Staff should be clear on who can grant exceptions to the renewal policy. There should be someone designated who will evaluate if there are other upcoming requests for the equipment, if this patron has reserved the equipment repeatedly (if they are monopolizing it), if there are other similar types of equipment that are still available for the public to use, or if the time frame that is requested is allowable. It may be that some shortened time frame can be accommodated.

**Returning technology.** The policy should state whether patrons can drop the borrowed equipment off at a branch library, put the equipment in a book drop, or return the equipment in person. Because of the need to check the items upon return and to have the patron and staff sign the form that verifies that all pieces have been returned in good condition, the UIUC Undergraduate Library has a strict policy about returning items. It states:

> Returning items: Items must be returned in person at the Technology (Loanable Technology) desk at the Undergraduate Library. You will need to verify (with the staff person) that each piece has been returned in good condition and sign the form again. **Failure to complete this process means that you did not return the item and you may be charged for it.** (http://www.library.illinois.edu/ugl/mc/loanable.html)

## Policy for Reserving Items

During the discussion on policies, your library may decide to offer patrons the option of reserving items ahead of time or to make equipment available only on a "first come, first served" basis. If you decide that advanced reservation is something your library wants to offer, you will need to implement an effective system of reservation; this will be further discussed in chapter 8.

At the UIUC Undergraduate Library, staff have learned to be vigilant to catch if a patron is continuously reserving a tech item for successive weeks, in order to prevent the patron from checking out a device for the whole semester. Patrons may reserve only one camera, not multiple cameras, unless they get permission for an exception. For example, they may be working on a particular project that requires two cameras for different viewpoints, or multiple items may be checked out to a teacher for a one- or two-day class session to demonstrate for students how to shoot video. These uses are approved on a case-by-case basis; approval is granted depending on the time of the semester and how many other items may be available for individuals to check out. The policy for UIUC is at http://www.library.illinois.edu/ugl/about/LoanableTechnology/techbooking.html.

Rice University's Fondred Library has a similar policy (https://library.rice.edu/services/dmc/about/policies/policies#DMC%20Reservation%20Procedure). They allow patrons a maximum number of two of the same type of equipment to check out at a time and restrict extended loans of any equipment. They also limit specific types of equipment to only one reservation per user per month.

## Privacy and Confidentiality Policies

All libraries should have in place privacy policies and procedures to ensure that confidential information in all formats is protected. The Family Educational Rights and Privacy Act (FERPA) is a federal law that protects the privacy of student education records (http://www.ed.gov/policy/gen/guid/fpco/ferpa/index.html). To safeguard privacy, the forms and checkout records for any loanable technology item must follow the same guidelines that are established for any library forms, records, or materials. Once an item is returned, the record or form should be deleted or shredded. Even if a family member comes in and asks to know what item their son, daughter, sister, or brother has checked out, a staff person cannot reveal any information (if that student is over eighteen years old). Even for school and public libraries, which have many patrons who are minors, the American Library Association recommends that libraries should make it clear to parents and guardians what the privacy and confidentiality policies are and should respect and protect the rights of minors to privacy. For additional guidance on developing a library privacy policy see the Privacy Tool Kit available at the American Library Association website (http://www.ala.org/advocacy/privacyconfidentiality/toolkitsprivacy/privacy). In addition to guidelines and samples for developing a policy, the tool kit includes a checklist of questions about privacy and confidentiality pertaining to collecting information, which can be useful for determining what information to keep, how long, how to destroy the information, and how to ensure safety.

Consistency by staff in adhering to the policies and guidelines is critical. By having policies stated in staff manuals and on websites, as well as communicated in meetings and in training sessions, employees cannot say that they were not aware of them. If policies are not consistently enforced, you run the risk of patrons becoming angry or frustrated if someone else is allowed to renew equipment more times than is permitted or if sometimes they are allowed to do so, but not always. In addition, errors can occur if one person deviates from the correct process, such as in equipment checks, record maintenance, overlapping reservations, or renewal conflicts. Familiarity with and review of the procedures should be incorporated in regular communications and training efforts by the library.

## TEXTBOX 7.5

## EXAMPLES OF TECHNOLOGY POLICIES

Following are examples of policies for circulating loanable technology, with some providing information about fines, damages, and personal data.

### Academic Libraries

- American University Library: http://www.american.edu/library/services/laptops.cfm
- Elmer E. Rasmuson Library at the University of Alaska–Fairbanks: http://library.uaf.edu/media
- Fondren Library at Rice University: https://library.rice.edu/services/dmc/about/policies/policies#DMC%20Reservation%20Procedure
- Greenwood Library at Longwood University: http://library.longwood.edu/about/policies/multimedia-lab-and-equipment-policy
- Lila D. Bunch Library at Belmont University: http://library.belmont.edu/services/index.html
- Munday Library at St. Edwards University: http://library.stedwards.edu/about/policies/gifts-and-donations
- Parkland College Library: http://parkland.libguides.com/content.php?pid=154127&sid=4235180
- Undergraduate Library at the University of Illinois at Urbana-Champaign, gift policy: http://www.library.illinois.edu/cmservices/gifts_policy.html; policy and procedure for checking out loanable technology: http://www.library.illinois.edu/ugl/mc/loanabletech/tech_checkout.html; and renewing technology: http://www.library.illinois.edu/ugl/about/LoanableTechnology/tech loan_renewing.html
- University of Arizona Libraries: http://www.library.arizona.edu/services/equipment-lending (click on each heading to read the specific policies)
- University of Tennessee–Knoxville, commons equipment loan period and fines: http://www.lib.utk.edu/access/equipment/; renewals: http://www.lib.utk.edu/access/renewals/
- Virginia Tech University Libraries: http://www.lib.vt.edu/artarch/ipad-policy.html
- Weigle Information Commons at the University of Pennsylvania: http://wic.library.upenn.edu/wicfacilities/lending.html
- Z. Smith Reynolds Library at Wake Forest University, iPad usage policy: http://zsr.wfu.edu/about/policies/ipad-usage; technology use policies: http://zsr.wfu.edu/about/policies/technology-use

### K–12 Schools

- Brewbaker Technology Magnet High School Library Media Center: http://www.brewtech.mps-al.org/?PageName=%27Library%27
- Paint Branch High School Media Center: https://www.montgomeryschoolsmd.org/schools/paintbranchhs/departments/media/index.aspx

### Public Libraries

- Bernardsville Public Library, audiobooks and e-readers: http://www.bernardsvillelibrary.org/audiobooks and http://www.bernardsvillelibrary.org/e-readers-loaded-and-ready-to-loan
- Cleveland Public Library TechCentral MakerSpace: http://www.cpl.org/TheLibrary/TechCentral/TechCentralMakerSpace.aspx
- Wells County Public Library: http://www.wellscolibrary.org/index.php/policies/services/#equipment

## Key Points

A library develops many policies for the use of its materials, services, and spaces. Although various aspects of a loanable technology program may be covered in these policies already, it will be necessary to review the existing policies and add in particular items that are unique to the technology items.

- Statements and policies should be included on the library's web page so that all patrons can view them and staff can refer to them when explaining expectations and procedures.
- A collection development policy should include the intent of the collection, target audience, scope of the collection, selection procedure, potential target number of items to maintain, procedures for donations, and collection maintenance. It should also include if there are categories within the collection, such as items for in-library use only or items that can circulate outside the library.
- Each library will need to determine if there should be restrictions on the equipment and how staff will communicate and enforce these restrictions (such as use of item, in-house use only, academic versus personal use, renewals or reservations of items, and number of items patrons can check out).
- Consistency by staff in adhering to the policies and guidelines is critical.

The next chapter provides more specifics about checking out and reserving equipment.

## References

Langworthy Public Library. 2014. Mission, Service and Technology Statements. Hope Valley, RI. http://langworthylibrary.org/?page_id=1507.

University of Alaska Fairbanks. 2014. Media Services. Elmer E. Rasmuson & BioSciences Libraries. http://library.uaf.edu/media.

University of Illinois at Urbana-Champaign. 2014. Media Commons Loanable Technology. http://www.library.illinois.edu/ugl/mc/loanable.html.

University of Illinois at Urbana-Champaign. 2012. Policy and Procedure for Checking out Loanable Technology at the Undergraduate Library. http://www.library.illinois.edu/ugl/mc/loanabletech/tech_checkout.html.

CHAPTER 8

# Reserving, Checking Out, and Checking In Loanable Technology

**IN THIS CHAPTER**

- ▷ Reserving technology
- ▷ Establishing equipment-loan agreement forms
- ▷ Preparing technology to be checked out
- ▷ Developing a check-in procedure
- ▷ Resolving situations in which equipment was damaged or pieces are missing
- ▷ Establishing procedures that prepare items to recirculate
- ▷ Collecting statistics
- ▷ Maintaining patron records

EVERY LIBRARY WILL HAVE its own process for checking out technology, including whether forms or agreements need to be filled out. As mentioned in the previous chapter, checking out technology can be based on policies and procedures for books, but policies may need to be modified for equipment based on cost, number of pieces, specialized loan periods, and whether or not there is some information that may need to be explained to the patron about the equipment. The first part of this chapter will address those processes, followed by a discussion of procedures that need to be followed when loanable technology items are returned.

## Reservations

In addition to patrons walking up to the desk and asking if a particular type of technology is available to be checked out, there is also a possibility that they may want to reserve an item beforehand. The process for reserving a technology item can be a bit more involved than the process for reserving books, especially if there are multiple items to be checked out. Additionally, reservations can be mediated or unmediated. Mediated reservations are ones in which a staff member is directly involved in setting up the reservation. These reservations could be made via an online form, in person, over the phone, or via e-mail, but they are not complete until a staff member enters the information into the reservation module, catalog, or system. Unmediated means patrons can reserve items in advance via an online catalog (much like reservations for books) or any other means that does not require staff to manually authorize the reservation. Regardless of whether the system is mediated or unmediated, the following questions should be discussed to make sure there are staff and policies in place for equipment reservations.

- Will patrons make their own reservations? If not, which staff members, volunteers, or student employees/volunteers will be allowed to make the reservation?
- Will you allow all items to be reserved or only some of them? Which ones and why? For example, if laptops cannot be reserved ahead of time, it will be important for staff to be able to explain the rationale for this (and it should also be included on the library's loanable technology web page).
- If mediated reservations are being used, during which hours of the day will staff be monitoring the requests? That information should be noted on the web page that provides the information about e-mailing, filling out a form, or calling in requests. This is important so that patrons understand it may take time for a staff member to review requests and provide a response.
- How far in advance must the reservations be made? Some libraries require a week's notice, and some require as little as a day's notice. You should also discuss how far in advance you will allow reservations. Is it at most a month in advance, or can they be made as much as three months in advance?
- Who will process the reservations and when? Are there staff who are charged with this task, and have they established a time of day to process the reservations and put them on the predetermined shelf for later pick up?
- Does processing the reservation include patron notification that the item is ready to be picked up? If so, who is responsible for that?
- How long is the grace period for a patron to pick up the item?
- Who will be responsible for monitoring and canceling unclaimed reservations?

Your library may decide to allow unmediated reservations for some things and mediated reservations for others. For instance, if you have some items that stay in the library and some that can be taken out of the library, you may consider mediating everything that can be used in the library and unmediating all technology used out of the library.

If your library does allow advance reservations, each day there should also be a dedicated staff member who prepares the items to be picked up, which could include putting the items in a designated place for pickup (such as a hold shelf) and contacting the patrons to let them know the item they booked is available for checkout. There should also be a staff member responsible for regular maintenance of the hold shelf, which includes

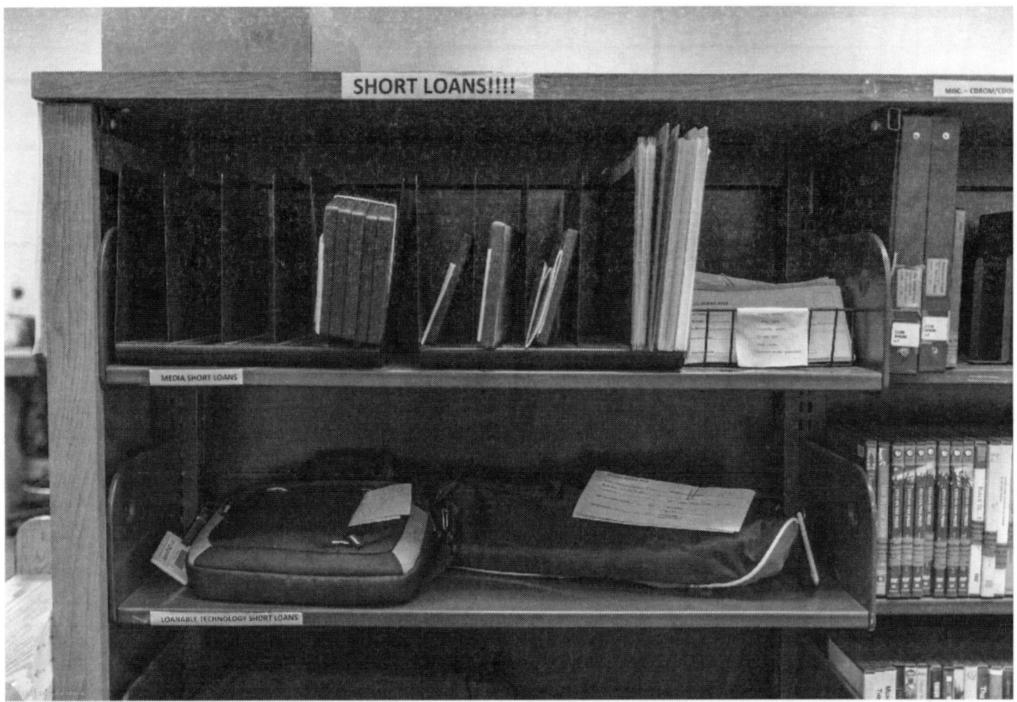


**Figure 8.1.** Equipment-Hold Shelves

canceling items that are not picked up and corresponding with patrons who either have not returned an item scheduled to go out or who are expecting to pick up an item that has not yet been returned.

You may also want to consider whether or not you will allow reservations to be made over the phone, online, via voicemail, or through e-mail. If any option other than in-person reservations is permitted, there could be delays due to the back-and-forth exchange between the patron and the staff member to determine what equipment is needed and for how long. Figure 8.1 illustrates a pick-up shelf that is designated for equipment that has been reserved. For consistency, a specific staff member should be responsible for maintenance of the shelf, for filling out paperwork, and for correspondence with patrons about their reservations.

**TEXTBOX 8.1**

Because of the expensive nature and high demand of loanable technology, it is recommended that the items be placed on a hold shelf that is behind the circulation desk. This will ensure greater security of the items until patrons pick them up.

## The Checkout Process

The basics of checking out technology to a patron may be similar from library to library (such as asking for a library card, scanning the items, and providing a due date), but there are additional steps that can vary significantly depending on the practices and preferences of each library. Various distinctions in the steps will be based on whether you use loan-agreement forms, whether the items are checked out through the circulation system, and whether you check for all the pieces before an item is circulated. As with any point of service, a streamlined checkout process is the goal.

Checkout practices will probably evolve over time, based on experience, policy changes, and new technology. Set a circulation procedure, and revise it as needed. Ask the point-of-service staff for recommendations, because they are the ones who are most often working with the process.

## Equipment-Loan Agreement Forms

An equipment-loan agreement form is a common practice at many libraries because the agreement often needs to be referred to when equipment is damaged or lost. Referring to the agreement in these situations is helpful because the patron has already agreed to be held responsible for returning the equipment in the condition in which it was checked out. Sometimes libraries require different forms for items that can be taken out of the library and those that can be used only in the library. Another common practice is to require loan agreements only for items that are valued over a certain amount, regardless of whether they can be used inside or outside the library.

Equipment-loan agreement forms take time to complete, both when checking out and returning items. This is especially true if a patron needs to fill out a separate form for each item, rather than filling out one form that covers all pieces being checked out. Another option that might work for some libraries is to have a one-time agreement that a patron fills out that covers all the items checked out over the course of a predetermined period of time (per month, per semester, per year). For school libraries it may be appropriate to do a one-time form at the beginning of the year for all the teachers, which will make the checkout process smoother and more streamlined during the rest of the year. Or perhaps it would be better to have each student sign an agreement form so that they understand the responsibility and liability of using library equipment. If you check out technology to students, you may need to have a parent or teacher also sign forms. Figure 8.2 is an example of an agreement form that covers the whole semester at a school library.

Having a specified time period to keep the forms on file is important so that staff can keep track of when a patron needs to renew the form or when it should be shredded to adhere to privacy guidelines, such as the Federal Educational Rights and Privacy Act (FERPA), which was discussed in chapter 7. The agreement renewal is a convenient time to remind the patron of responsibility and liability. If an equipment-loan form is not used at your library, decide on how you and the patron will agree that all pieces have been returned correctly.

## Checking the Item for All the Pieces

Before the patron takes the item out of the library, it is good to have a process established for checking the equipment to make sure all the pieces are present. This may involve double-checking against a list or picture included with the main item, or it could mean that the pieces are gathered together at the point of service (if they are all kept separate). Whatever your system, it is important that both the staff and the patron are in agreement about the pieces that are checked out. This will be especially important in the event of a lost or damaged item.

**Your Library Name**
**Equipment Loan Agreement**

Contact information:

Phone: 123-4567

Email:technology@yourlibrary.com

***Borrower Information***

| LAST NAME: | FIRST NAME: |
|---|---|
| Campus ID Number (if different from library barcode): | Library Barcode: |

***Description of Equipment***

| Make/Model: | **Replacement cost of equipment:** $ __**Borrower Initial** |
|---|---|

***Terms of Loan and statement of liability***

The library is not responsible for any damage that may occur on equipment while it is in care of the borrower. __**Borrower Initial**

Overdue fines of $5.00 per hour begin accruing immediately after the due time. __**Borrower Initial**

The terms of loan and statement of liability described in this document cover any and all times the equipment is loaned out to the borrower between the dates of _________ and __________.

*I have read and accepted the terms of loan and statement of liability above.*

Borrower Signature date Staff Name/Signature date

This form will remain on file in the Undergraduate Library until ____________.

**Figure 8.2.** Example of an Equipment-Loan Form for the Whole Semester

## Choosing a Due Time

Although it may be fine in many libraries to have the due date calculated based on when the item is checked out (like a book), you may want to consider altering this for loanable technology. Rather than allowing equipment to be due at any hour of the day, having a standard time that every technology item is due can be a good idea. It may be one hour before your library closes (to give time for the check-in process), or if your library has extended hours, you may think about choosing a consistent time such as 6:00 p.m. or 9:00 p.m. This is especially helpful if a patron is waiting for an item to be returned and can plan to return after the time that it is due back. Whatever you decide about the due time, make sure to communicate that to the patron and have it printed or stamped someplace with the equipment that is checked out.

## Keeping Track of the Agreement Form

If you do require agreement forms to be signed, then there needs to be a way to keep track of them until items are returned. This largely depends on the type of form you use. If you use Microsoft Word documents or a web form and then print forms out, it is possible you will have an alphabetical file or binder in which the forms are kept until the items are returned. Figure 8.3 is an example of a binder used to hold agreement forms while items

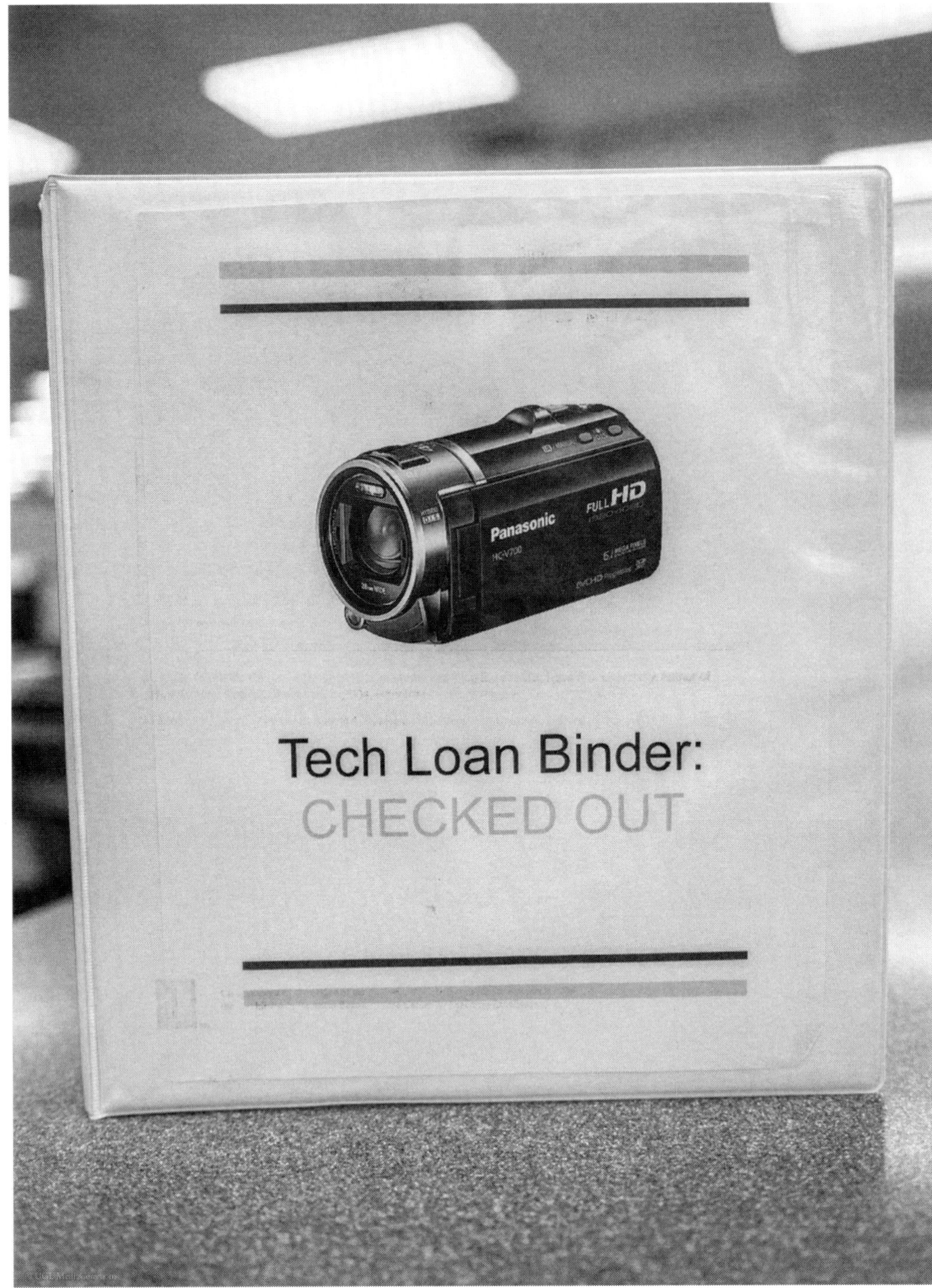


**Figure 8.3.** "Checked Out" Binder

are checked out. After items are returned and accounted for, the forms are shredded or locked in a place that is not accessible to the public (for privacy reasons).

If you have been able to develop a database that prepopulates a form for an item, it will be important to have a process for deleting patron information upon return of the item. If you have agreement forms that can be kept on file for an extended period of time for types of equipment that may be checked out periodically, like laptops or tablets, or if you have a database system that holds patron information for a certain period of time, then at the end of that period someone will need to verify that the information has been deleted.

**TEXTBOX 8.2**

Establish policies and procedures for what types of forms will be used, how the forms will be stored (database, binders, file cabinets), for how long, and how and when they will be deleted. Just as with other patron records, you will need a process to manually shred or delete individual patron transactions after items have been returned, if they have been returned in acceptable condition.

## Renewing Equipment

If your library has decided to allow renewals, there needs to be a process in place for how to grant renewals. Renewals are similar to reservations in that they may be mediated or unmediated. If renewals at your library are unmediated, patrons will be able to renew their equipment online. Unmediated renewals can get tricky if your library allows advance reservations because your library circulation system might authorize renewals up to the time that the item is reserved in advance for the next patron to pick up. If the patron who has the item checked out brings it back late, the person who was expecting to pick it up may be disappointed. If you have mediated renewals, the person authorizing the renewal will be able to build in a cushion of time if another patron has the item reserved.

**TEXTBOX 8.3**

Recommendation: Have at least one full day and two nights between when an item is due and when it is scheduled to go back out. This ensures that there is time for the item to be checked in properly and possibly charged or data-wiped before the next patron checks it out.

If your library allows renewals and also requires an equipment-loan agreement to be filled out, it is a good idea to indicate on the agreement form if the item has been renewed. Whether or not your library allows advance reservations or requires equipment-loan forms, it is important to think critically and practically about how the process will work. Adding the renewal to the original agreement form can save future confusion when the item is checked in by alerting the staff to the revised due date.

As with the checkout process, there are certain procedures that need to be followed when loanable technology items are returned. In many cases, the check-in process will be similar to doing the checkout process backward, but in some cases there will be different procedures.

## Item Check-In Procedure

When a patron returns loanable technology, there are several steps that should be followed before discharging the equipment. These steps will vary, depending on whether your library has equipment-loan forms and whether it has a station set up to review equipment that has been returned. Regardless of whether or not there is a form, the equipment should be checked to make sure it has all the pieces and is in good condition.

## Equipment-Loan Form

If there is an equipment-loan form, the return portion should be filled out and the technology item can be discharged from the patron's account. Discuss with your colleagues whether or not to have a second check of the technology item before it is returned to the storage cabinet. This could be another student or a dedicated staff person, but the goal would be to double-check that all the pieces are there and undamaged. A procedure like this would be especially helpful for libraries whose loanable technology desks are busy and whose loanable technology staff feels rushed to complete transactions because of other patrons waiting to be helped.

## Checking the Condition of Returned Equipment

Make sure all the pieces were returned. If all the pieces have not been returned, or if one or more appears to be damaged, it is best to catch this while the patron is still standing at the point of service. This allows for two things: the patron can provide an explanation, and the patron and the staff can gather information on what exactly is missing or damaged. If all the pieces are present and appear undamaged, the full check-in process can proceed.

A process should be in place for what to do when a patron returns an item that is damaged or has missing pieces. Billing policies and procedures with the patron will be discussed in chapter 9, but there should be a procedure in place for what to do to alert the billing staff that something is awry. It can be tricky to discuss with the patron what happened while they are standing at the circulation desk, but as soon as the damage is noticed, the patron should be asked politely if they know anything about it. Whether the patron claims to know anything about the damage or not, the next step is to communicate the problem to the person who will resolve the problem.

Notification could take the form of a standard equipment-problem report or a verbal notification if the staff person is available. Figure 8.4 is an example of an equipment-problem report form, which can also be kept for recording statistics.

## Equipment-Problem Form

Resolving issues of damaged equipment or missing pieces may involve patron contact, evaluation of current procedures, or replacement of the damaged or missing item, so it is important that whatever is known about the situation is conveyed to the staff person who will resolve the issue.

## Patron Confidentiality and Loan Agreement Forms

After the item has been discharged and checked (once or twice, depending on your procedure), any record of the transaction needs to be deleted. Because of patron privacy, many libraries do not keep records of patron transactions in any format, including within databases after material has been returned. A good practice is to shred any paperwork that links a patron with an item that he or she has previously checked out. The end goal,

**Equipment Problem Report**

Date: _________ Your name: _______________ Supervisor: ___________________

o Media Viewing Station o Loanable Technology o Group Room o Gaming Center

Equipment ____________________________________________________________

Barcode: _________________________ copy #: ______

Does Patron want a reply? Patron Name: ______________________________________

Barcode: _________________________ Email: ____________________@Illinois.edu

Is the item "In Process"? Yes No Is the item Discharged? Yes No

**Staff use only:**

Patron notified: ___/___

Staff initials: _________

**Tell me about the problem** (please use as much detail as possible):

**Staff use only:**

Initials: _____ Date: _____

**Equipment Problem Report**

Date: _________ Your name: _______________ Supervisor: ___________________

o Media Viewing Station o Loanable Technology o Group Room o Gaming Center

Equipment ____________________________________________________________

Barcode: _________________________ copy #: ______

Does Patron want a reply? Patron Name: ______________________________________

Barcode: _________________________ Email: ____________________@Illinois.edu

Is the item "In Process"? Yes No Is the item Discharged? Yes No

**Staff use only:**

Patron notified: ___/___

Staff initials: _________

**Tell me about the problem** (please use as much detail as possible):

**Staff use only:**

Initials: _____ Date: _____

**Figure 8.4.** Equipment-Problem Form

whether you use paper forms or a database, is to appropriately wipe personally identifiable information from the record. For many libraries, this could mean shredding paper forms or deleting data from a database, but you may have another way of destroying the information that works for you. Ideally, the only pieces of information gathered and kept about the transaction will be for statistical purposes and will not include patron data.

The length of time that specific transaction information is kept will vary from library to library depending on the method of storing data and compiling statistics. If your library uses paper forms, perhaps the forms will be placed in a file folder or drawer, or maybe a binder, until the statistical information can be gathered.

## Preparing Equipment for Recirculation

In some instances, the equipment used will need to be charged or have its data wiped before it can circulate again. Removing data protects the privacy of the person who had it checked out and is a courtesy to the patron who will check it out next. Some of these policies were discussed in chapter 7 and are further detailed here because of how intertwined these polices are. It is best to think about how data will be removed and have a process in place before the item is lent out the first time. Discuss and create a process for the following:

- Whose responsibility is it to charge or delete data from the device? Is it an appropriate student task or will there be a full-time staff person dedicated to this job? If a full-time staff member does it, are there times that the equipment might be returned but not available?
- How long will the item be unavailable before it returns to the circulating pool?
- How will other staff members be alerted to the fact that the item is not currently available for circulation? Think about changing the status to "In Process" or "Circulation Review" or something that indicates it is not missing or broken, just currently unavailable, until the item returns to circulation. Whose responsibility will it be to change the status of the equipment?
- Where will items be put that are waiting to be charged or have data wiped?
- Where will the charging station be?
- Will the items need to be secured if the library closes while they're charging?

As with any procedure, each library should develop its own process based on current practices and staffing levels.

Finally, when the items have been checked for pieces, wiped, and charged, they can be returned to the cabinet or shelf to be circulated again. All statuses that indicate the item is unavailable should be removed to communicate to all staff members that the item is ready to be checked out.

When an item is returned, it should be checked first for damage or missing pieces and then prepared for the next circulation. Consistency in practice for how staff discharge and handle equipment that is returned is very important.

## Key Points

Setting up a smooth and efficient checkout process requires thoughtful planning and procedures. Following are some of the main points addressed in this chapter that will help make the checkout and check-in processes function seamlessly:

- Using an equipment-loan agreement form helps clarify circulation and return procedures.
- Consider allowing advance reservations for circulating technology.
- Streamline the checkout and check-in processes as much as possible.
- Check equipment for damage when it is returned.
- Develop a plan for addressing damaged and missing pieces.
- Keep patron records private.
- Keep circulation and problem statistics.

Chapter 9 discusses correspondence with patrons and provides suggestions for setting up billing policies and procedures.

CHAPTER 9

# Billing, Fines, and Communication with Patrons

**IN THIS CHAPTER**

- ▷ Billing department practices and guidelines
- ▷ Practical steps for implementing your policies
- ▷ When to initiate contact with the patron regarding loaned equipment
- ▷ Tips for mitigating fines

THIS CHAPTER WILL discuss how to handle issues that arise with loanable technology equipment as a result of the items being lent, which includes both patron-initiated contact with the library and library-initiated contact with the patron. As mentioned briefly in chapter 8, there should be a designated person or department who responds to inquiries about fines, fees, and damages.

## The Billing Department

Depending on the type and size of your library, the billing department may look and operate very differently from that of other libraries. In a school library the fines and fees may be collected by the office staff or in the library itself by the library staff. An academic library may either collect fines on location or have the fines applied to the patron's school account. Public libraries may allow payment at the circulation desk or have a separate department on location to accept fine payments. Perhaps your library does not charge fines, or perhaps your circulation staff are not trained to investigate the charges. Regardless of how your library handles fine inquiries, the process needs to include options for how library staff will respond to inquiries about loanable equipment fines, fees, and damages.

The "billing department" in this chapter will refer to the person, persons, or department that resolves issues related to equipment return. These issues could range from fine inquiries to damaged equipment. Your library may decide to continue with the same practices of billing for other materials, so you could follow those guidelines. Review those guidelines and see if they also could apply or be adapted for loanable technology. The sidebar contains some general billing questions that were used at the University of Illinois to help set up the billing practices for the loanable technology program.

Billing practices for other items, like books or media, may be adapted to suit loanable equipment situations, but it is highly unlikely that exact procedures will be the same. Further discussion of some of these questions and options are included in the next sections. You will need to establish fixed procedures and practices for how the library corresponds with patrons regarding billing.

### TEXTBOX 9.1

### BILLING QUESTIONS FOR LOANABLE TECHNOLOGY

The following questions should be discussed to determine practices for loanable technology. Place the questions and responses in a single document so that the process is known and followed consistently.

How does your library notify its patrons of fines and fees?

- Via an automated e-mail before an item is due, when an item is due, or after an item is due?
- Via an individual who sends out the notification?

How will your library accept inquiries about fines and fees?

- Does your library discuss fees in person, over the phone, or via e-mail inquiries?
- Is there a separate department that handles fine inquiries?

Who is qualified to answer questions about fines and fees?

- Only designated individuals with access to patron accounts, who can interpret how and why the fines were levied?
- Anyone in the department?
- What is the established time period for responding to patron inquiries? Within a day, two days, etc.?

Where will fines and fees be paid?

- At any library location?
- At the main office?
- Through some established third party?

Which method(s) of payment will be accepted?

## Correspondence with Patrons

Any correspondence with patrons, whether in person, via e-mail, or over the phone, should contain accurate and complete information, especially when it involves library fines and fees. Two types of communications that library staff will encounter for billing are patron-initiated and library-initiated. These are discussed below.

### Patron-Initiated Correspondence with the Library

The correspondence a library receives from its patrons is highly dependent on the type of communication that is sent about items that the patron has checked out. Many times patron-initiated correspondence with the library is the result of a notification received, although sometimes it is because the patron suspects they have returned an item late and are checking to see if there are consequences.

**TEXTBOX 9.2**

**COMMON TYPES OF PATRON-INITIATED CONTACT WITH LIBRARY**

- To claim an item has been returned
- To inquire about fines
- To inquire about circulation and overdue policies
- To check the status of an account

Patron-initiated correspondence can, at times, escalate into uncomfortable situations. It is best to have a member of the billing staff respond to these situations because these individuals are trained to interpret fines and will have the authority and necessary library-system permissions to mitigate and resolve the situations. If a patron inquires about charges in person or on the phone, and there is no one who can respond to the situation immediately, the billing department should also have an e-mail address through which it can be contacted. Having only a member of the billing staff be able to communicate with a patron about fines and fees, rather than anyone on staff, helps maintain consistency in responses. E-mail communication is especially effective because it gives the billing staff extra time to investigate and the communication is documented.

### Library-Initiated Correspondence with Patrons

Any time the library sends correspondence to a patron, whether it is in the form of an automatically generated notice or a manually drafted e-mail, it is considered library-initiated patron contact. Common types of library-initiated e-mail correspondence with patrons are in textbox 9.3. Sometimes these e-mails prompt a written response from the patron, and it is through this correspondence that situations can be resolved.

When a patron responds to these notices, it is critical to make sure that all the billing staff follow the best practices that your library sets up so all patrons receive fair treatment and a uniform response.

### TEXTBOX 9.3

#### COMMON TYPES OF LIBRARY-INITIATED PATRON CONTACT

- Notice that a hold is ready to be picked up
- Courtesy notice
- Overdue notice
- Notice of amount owed
- Notice of account suspension

## Using Templates and Scripts

When responding to patrons, it is best for all billing staff to respond to inquiries using similar language. Develop a script for use when explaining fines in person or over the phone, and use e-mail templates that explain the most common inquiries. Because each situation is nuanced, the templates and scripts may need to be slightly modified on the fly, but the structure and information should be the same. See textbox 9.4 for an example of an e-mail template and textbox 9.5 for suggestions about what information to include in a template.

### TEXTBOX 9.4

#### EXPLANATION OF A FINE

Dear PATRON,
Thank you for contacting us. According to our records, the fines on your account are for the following items:

DATE CHARGED TO ACCOUNT:

ITEM
Checked out to you DD/MM/YY, due DD/MM/YY, returned DD/MM/YY
Charge: $xxx

ITEM
Checked out to you DD/MM/YY, due DD/MM/YY, returned DD/MM/YY
Charge: $xxx

Overdue fees for loanable technology are $xx/day, including partial days. Do these charges seem correct to you?

Please let us know if you have any further questions or concerns.

Thank you,
YOUR LIBRARY

## TEXTBOX 9.5

### TIPS FOR TEMPLATES AND SCRIPTS

- Use a standard greeting, which includes thanking the patron for their correspondence.
- Explain the situation from the library's standpoint.
- Mention any relevant library policies and include a link to them, if available.
- Stick to the facts and do not include superfluous information.
- Include in your salutation an invitation to continue correspondence if the patron needs further clarification.

## When a Library Should Contact a Patron

Since the equipment that your library lends will probably be in high demand, you may want to think about being more proactive in advocating its timely return. In addition to the generic system-generated courtesy and overdue notices, you may want to send out manually generated e-mail reminders at different intervals that contain stronger language. Your policies for late materials will already be determined, so the manually generated e-mail reminders will simply spell out the policy in more specific, and stronger, terms. For instance, if your library's courtesy notice goes out three days before the due date and the overdue notices go out one day and five days past the due date, you may want to send out a manual notice seven days and ten days past the due date. It is also a good idea to create a generic circulation e-mail account for manually generated notices so that responses can be monitored by staff members but not sent to any specific individual. This is especially helpful because it keeps all the correspondence in one inbox that can be accessed by all billing staff. Previous interactions with patrons are searchable and all library staff have access to the inbox to resolve situations, regardless of who is in or out of the office at any given time.

Your library may want to develop a stronger incentive for return if an item is overdue for a specified number of days, such as suspending the borrower's privileges until they return the item that is overdue. Run a report one to three times each week to keep track of which items may become overdue to the point that you want to more actively pursue their return. For the Undergraduate Library at the University of Illinois at Urbana-Champaign (UIUC), this point is ten days overdue. Textboxes 9.6 and 9.7 are examples of manually generated notices that can be modified depending on the situation.

Libraries should also contact patrons with a manually generated notice if a returned item has been damaged or if an item is missing one of the pieces that circulates with it. The communication should ask for an explanation and give the patron options to resolve the situation. As discussed in chapter 8, it is a good practice to use equipment-loan agreement forms. This is especially beneficial in cases of items that are not returned or are returned with a missing or damaged piece. The equipment-loan agreement form is considered by the library to be a contract and indicates the fines and fees for items that are missing or damaged. The patron is responsible for upholding his or her end of the agreement.

## TEXTBOX 9.6

## MANUALLY GENERATED OVERDUE NOTICE

Dear PATRON,
It has been brought to our attention that an item on your account, ITEM, is overdue. Overdue charges for one-week loanable technology items are $x/day, including partial days.

Once these items have been overdue for ten days, they will be declared "Lost" and your account will be charged a replacement value and an overdue fine for each item. The charges on your account will be:

ITEM lost-item replacement value: $xxx
ITEM overdue fee: $xxx

Total charges that will be added to your account: $xxx

If you do not respond to this email or return the item by THREE DAYS AFTER TODAY, your library account will be blocked. When your library account is blocked, you will be unable to check out or renew any items from YOUR LIBRARY SYSTEM libraries. Please return this item at your earliest convenience to the loanable technology desk.

Please let us know if you have questions or concerns.

Thank you,
YOUR LIBRARY

## TEXTBOX 9.7

## MANUALLY GENERATED NOTICE OF LIBRARY ACCOUNT SUSPENSION

Dear PATRON,
We are contacting you because you have not responded to our attempt to contact you on DATE regarding the ITEM you have checked out.

As of DAY, DATE, your library account will be suspended. This means that you will be unable to check out or renew items from YOUR LIBRARY SYSTEM libraries.

To rectify this situation, please return the item to the YOUR LIBRARY Loanable Technology Desk as soon as possible. When the item is returned, we will request that your account be unsuspended and we will refund the lost-item replacement fines (totaling $TOTAL). If you no longer have the item, or don't know where it is, we would be happy to outline our replacement policy. Please return this item to the YOUR LIBRARY loanable technology desk at your earliest convenience.

Please let us know if you have further questions or concerns.

Thank you,
YOUR LIBRARY

## Tips for Mitigating Fines

Even when policies and procedures are clearly stated, there will be instances when patrons want to discuss a fine. In many libraries they can do this directly (in person or by phone) with an individual who is in charge of billing operations. However, it may be that your library cannot always have an expert in billing available all the hours that the library is open. In those instances, other options could be established. Following are some suggestions for those options, as well as some best practices for working with patrons who may be upset and for responding to fines via e-mail.

### Tips for Mitigating Fines via Phone or in Person

Often patrons will call the library or come in person to ask about a notice they received about a late item. Some libraries may expect any staff person at the desk to handle these situations, whereas others may let the patron know that there is a designated individual or department who handles this and refer them. A process that has been effective at the Undergraduate Library at the University of Illinois is to require all billing queries for loanable technology to be directed to a single e-mail account. Although many patrons want to talk to a "real person," this e-mail process has been developed to allow designated billing staff an opportunity to check the patron's record in private, investigate the situation, and respond appropriately. Even if the patron comes in person or calls the library to talk about the notice, they are still given the e-mail address and told that they will be contacted within a day. If the process is to refer a patron, it will still be important to listen to the patron and politely refer them. If the person at the desk needs to assist, the following are some suggestions to help an upset patron.

- Keep calm and smile. Agitated patrons may be calmed by your serene and assured presence.
- Listen to what the patron has to say and use active listening techniques such as nodding, clarifying what you hear the patron saying, and acknowledging what you hear them say.
- Be able to back up what you say with library policy and bring it up on the library website so the patron is also able to view it.
- Use gentle phrases like "It looks like [insert situation] happened. Does this seem correct to you?" and "Let me see if I understand you correctly. [Repeat back what the patron just told you]." This will help the patron know you are listening to them.
- Tell them how you can help them, even if it is to direct them to another individual and apologize for the inconvenience.
- If the patron becomes irate, if your efforts are not working, or if the patron does not seem to be listening to your explanation, offer to get someone else. Even if the other staff person says the same thing you have been trying to tell the patron, there is something about having someone else explain it that calms patrons down.
- Reiterate to patrons what you both have discussed and what the next steps are for this process.

### Tips for Mitigating Fines via E-mail

E-mail correspondence can be both advantageous and disadvantageous. Advantages include the documentation of communication and the ability for staff to send e-mails day or night. A disadvantage is that sometimes a patron may not reply promptly or a patron may become aggravated if they do not get an immediate response. Following are some tips for e-mail correspondence.

- Respond to inquiries in a timely manner. Usually one to two business days is an appropriate time frame for a first response, even if the response is just a message that says something like "Thank you for your patience. We are looking into this matter for you and will respond shortly."
- Do not, however, feel obligated to respond to each inquiry immediately. Waiting a day may bring greater clarity to the situation and other ideas for an appropriate resolution.
- Make sure you have all the facts before you respond. Sometimes this means waiting an extra day before you respond, but it is far better to respond with a well-informed e-mail than to have to send a correction.
- Be fair, but be sensitive. Some situations will be similar, but each situation is unique. For instance, if your policy is to never forgive fines because of illness, stick to that policy for everyone. Or, if you waive any patron's first fine as a courtesy, be consistent regardless of the patron's tone in the e-mail.
- Use exceptions sparingly. Make sure the situation is indeed exceptional. If you find yourself granting the same exception over and over, you may want to consider making it a policy.
- Be succinct without omitting important details or being terse. Too many words will muddle the message of the e-mail.
- Be specific when communicating interdepartmentally. If your billing department has more than one staff person and you are discussing a certain situation, it is OK to use specifics for greater clarity.
- Read the e-mail through one last time as though you were the patron reading this information for the first time. Use the opportunity to correct anything that may not be clear.
- Create templates to save time and to help with consistency in responses.
- Know your limits. Your time is a valuable resource and if one person or situation is taking up too much of it, perhaps it would be better to pass off the situation to your supervisor or a "fine mitigation board," if you have one.

## Maintaining Anonymity

Depending on the size and structure of your library, you will want to discuss among your colleagues whether the person who resolves issues for patrons should maintain anonymity. Maintaining the anonymity of the billing staff ensures that one staff member will not be singled out to resolve problems and also allows for collaboration among all the staff on any situation. Anonymity might be a good idea for your billing department if you want to take the personal association out of what could be uncomfortably agitated situations. A smaller library or a library with fewer patrons may have difficulty maintaining the anonymity of the staff person who resolves equipment fines simply because there are fewer library staff.

For instance, at the UIUC Undergraduate Library, the people working in the billing department are unknown to the patrons. When a patron inquires about a fine or fee on their account, they are given an e-mail address and all correspondence about the situation takes place via e-mail. All e-mail history is kept so that the billing staff can track what is said to the patron regarding the situation and can refer to old e-mails when resolving new situations with different patrons or continuing situations with the same patron.

## Key Points

Addressing patron inquiries regarding fines and initiating patron contact regarding overdue, lost, missing, or damaged items should be handled prudently. The following points can help provide consistency and fairness in the billing process:

- Develop billing best practices
- Use a template or script when corresponding with patrons
- Make sure the billing department has an e-mail address
- Maintain an anonymous billing department

Chapter 10 departs from the day-to-day operation of a loanable technology program to discuss training the staff to help support patrons in the use of the equipment.

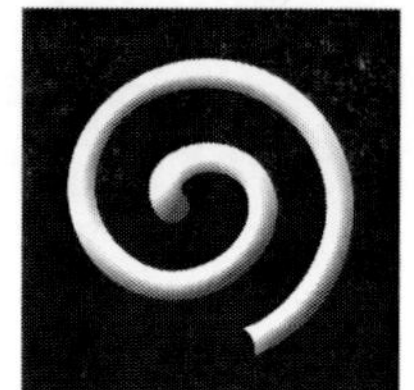

# Training and Support

**IN THIS CHAPTER**

- ▷ Training all staff in basic functions and troubleshooting of technology
- ▷ Training patrons about which technology items are available, which items best fit their needs, and how to check them out
- ▷ Training technology staff in more advanced troubleshooting
- ▷ Supporting the loanable technology program through a variety of staff expertise

ONCE EQUIPMENT IS prepared for circulation, attention should be given to setting up training for staff so that they can, in turn, train patrons on the checkout processes and equipment. The first part of this chapter discusses suggestions for training staff. Once training is complete, promotion for the program can occur, which can also be a form of training. The last part of the chapter provides guidance for training patrons in the use and care of equipment that they check out and ideas for supporting technology training.

## Educating Circulation Desk Employees about the Loanable Technology Collection

Circulation desk employees could include volunteers, students, and part-time or full-time employees. At some libraries, employees who work at the loanable technology desk might not work at other circulation points of service, but at other libraries, employees are cross-trained in all areas of circulation. Whichever scenario best describes your situation, the library staff need to be able to provide knowledgeable assistance at the point of service in the area of loanable technology. Therefore, it is necessary for the staff to be trained not only in circulation procedures, but also in basic usage and operation of the equipment.

## Types of Training

Depending on the size of your loanable technology collection and staff, your training models will differ. One suggestion is to have a weekly training session in which employees are introduced to a new piece of technology or a new function of equipment they have already learned about. Training could include videos, quizzes or assessments, demonstrations, assignments, presentations, or other forms of training. If in an academic environment, check to see if it is possible for you to use your institution's online course-management system (e.g., Moodle or Blackboard). Enrolling your staff in a training course allows you to keep the content on the site and reveal it as needed.

## General Supervisor Training

As previously mentioned, circulation desk employees and supervisors may, depending on your situation, be the employees responsible for operating the loanable technology desk. It could also be the case that these same individuals are cross-trained in other departments that involve technology. Since loanable technology is inherently a technology-centric enterprise, it is important for everyone who works with the technology to undergo a level of training that will allow them to better facilitate the activities at the loanable technology desk. This can result in the need for different levels of technology-based training, depending on responsibilities. This section on training will focus on the supervisor designation and what is specifically important for a supervisor to understand for a loanable technology program to function efficiently.

Generally, the supervisor training should be conducted by someone knowledgeable in technology or experienced in using technology. This person may be the school librarian, the director of the library, a staff person with interest in the area, someone from the information technology department, or even someone from the community. Additional suggestions for resource assistance for training will be discussed later in the chapter.

A major topic of training for library staff should be to cover the functions and use of the equipment in the program. Even a basic level of knowledge about the operation of the technology that is available will greatly improve the effectiveness of the loanable technology desk by allowing supervisors to address commonly occurring patron questions and solve simple equipment-support concerns. This level of training does not need to be advanced or extremely detailed, but it should cover the first layer of use and questions often asked by patrons while checking out equipment at the loanable tech desk. Options for this training may include quick guides, videos, and hands-on demonstrations.

### TEXTBOX 10.1

### TYPES OF EQUIPMENT INFORMATION USEFUL FOR SUPERVISORS TO KNOW AND UNDERSTAND

- How to operate key buttons on a digital video camera, including power, record/pause, and zoom
- How to replace memory cards and batteries
- How to record to a specific data source
- How to retrieve data

SONY
For easy set-up of Bloggie Live, visit the
www.sony.net/start/bloggie

Web
Instruction Manual

bloggie Live
Shoot, Connect and Share
View images on multiple devices and share with friends.
MHS-TS55


**Figure.10.1.** Screenshot of a Quick-Start Guide

Some excellent resources to use for the beginning trainer are the quick guides, or getting-started guides, that usually accompany tech items (see figure 10.1). These guides are designed specifically to help a user get started in a minimal amount of time and understand the basic functions of the equipment.

For those libraries that have designated someone to train the staff on loanable technology and loanable technology equipment, a face-to-face demonstration of technology can be useful. The University of Illinois at Urbana-Champaign program offers these technology demonstrations or "Tech Talks" during weekly staff meetings. The time needed is minimal, usually around ten minutes. This is just long enough to cover basic functions. The following questions are addressed in a "Tech Talk" that introduces a new piece of technology:

- What is the use and function of the device?
- Who is the contact to troubleshoot tech issues?
- What might a patron ask about this item?
- What might a patron need to know about this item?
- Does the patron need anything external to use the technology?
- Is the patron required to provide anything to use the equipment, such as a memory card or battery?

Once your staff is familiar with the basic operations of an item, and depending on the size of your staff, you may want to assign specific individuals to receive additional training about basic troubleshooting. This will help distribute the workload for maintaining the loanable technology and will help staff be better able to assist patrons at the desk. For instance, Flip Ultra Video Cameras will sometimes display a message that they are full but will not display any files. There is a hidden trash folder that is displayed and can be deleted only when the Flip camera is plugged into a computer. This is a process that could be performed by trained staff at the circulation desk so that the patron can immediately use the item. Depending on the size of your staff, it may not be beneficial to train everyone in basic troubleshooting.

## Educating Patrons about the Loanable Technology Collection

Once staff are competent in the various equipment and procedures, they can communicate this information to patrons. Many unique policies, procedures, and expectations accompany the process of loaning out technology, as compared to books. This section will describe some proactive ways that library staff can help patrons learn these policies and procedures, as well as how to set reasonable expectations for the program.

### Promoting a Loanable Technology Program to Patrons

One way to educate patrons about a loanable technology program is through promotion efforts. Whenever a library adds a new service, it is important to communicate the service and specifics so that patrons understand who is eligible and the policies and procedures for access. Marketing efforts also constitute a form of training. The extent of your marketing efforts will depend on resources, both personnel and budgetary, at your library. See textbox 10.2 for some suggestions for marketing your loanable technology program.

**TEXTBOX 10.2**

**WAYS TO PUBLICIZE AND PROMOTE THE LOANABLE TECHNOLOGY PROGRAM**

- Banners (in the library to advertise the loanable technology desk)
- Brochures
- Commercials (ads on buses, Facebook, Twitter)
- Newsletters (excerpts included in community, school, or library newsletters—both print and online)
- Listservs and e-mail blitzes
- Posters (on bulletin boards at community establishments, schools, departments)
- Public announcements (radio, television, social media)
- Tours and presentations (either at the library or on the road)
- Video promotions (showing the equipment, how to use it, and potential results)
- Website (library, school, and community)
- Workshops (either at the library or on the road)
- Word of mouth

### How to Determine What a Patron Needs

Most patrons will have a specific end goal in mind but might not know which technology item is best to help them achieve that goal. Information that will help them make a decision should be accessible in many places, including websites, catalog records, and documentation that can readily be accessed by library staff.

In addition to the information that should be included on the website (discussed in chapter 7), there could also be a link to an infographic, LibGuide, video clip, or other document to help patrons determine which piece of technology would be appropriate for their project. For instance, you could have a link that says "Help Me Choose a Camera" that would lead the patron to the camera infographic, which would be a series of questions that will help guide the patron to the most appropriate camera for their project. In a school or university environment, students may be trying to find the best equipment to complete a classroom assignment. In that case, a class-specific LibGuide with suggested equipment choices would be appropriate. Or, if the library is aware that a particular project is coming up, a librarian or staff member could present the equipment in the classroom or have the instructor put suggested equipment on the syllabus. The Northwest Arkansas Community College Library has put together a LibGuide for explaining what equipment is available and how to check it out (http://guides.nwacc.edu/content.php?pid=541133&sid=4451490). It also includes information about what services and trainings are offered to patrons.

Patrons also learn which equipment to use through word of mouth. Although this method works great for marketing and may be useful in many cases, library staff should be able to answer basic selection questions at the point of checkout.

## Using the Technology

When patrons leave the library with a loanable technology item, they need to be equipped with instructions about how to use the item. As discussed in chapter 6, one of the things that should be included with the item when it circulates is a quick-start guide. Even if a staff person gives a quick demo at the circulation desk before the patron leaves, the patron may need something to refer to later on. Links to the user manual should also be readily available (if the user manual is not circulated with the item) in multiple places—in the catalog record, on the website, and via a QR code somewhere within the item's package.

## Procedures

Patrons also need to be notified of any special procedures associated with loanable technology. Special procedures can include, but are not limited to, where, how, and when to return loanable technology items. For instance, if loanable technology should be returned to a certain service point or particular branch in the library system, this needs to be made known. This information should be on the website, on the agreement form (if you have one), and on the materials that circulate with the item.

## Common Questions about Equipment

Like many other user-based service points, you will find that patrons often ask very similar questions about service policies or equipment functions. These questions can be an excellent opportunity to focus training. This approach can be extremely useful in the implementation and expansion of loanable technology. You might survey the staff for the most common technology-related questions that occur at the desk and their responses. This provides a baseline understanding of the types of communication between patron and staff. It can also provide information for documentation, such as a frequently asked question sheet or other documentation to assist in responses to technology related questions.

### Patron and Other External Training

Basic equipment training for staff is essential in order to help patrons become familiar with the equipment and to answer those commonly asked questions. If you have a staff person or volunteer who has more advanced training in audio and video production and editing, you may be able to offer workshops, consultations, or demonstrations to the public.

## Training Groups of Patrons

Group trainings can help maximize time for trainers. These could include classroom demonstrations, demonstrations at community centers or other gatherings, workshops, or other scheduled trainings in the library. Refer to textbox 10.3 for suggestions about how to set up a group training time. It may not be possible to have equipment for each person in the group to use, so the trainer will need to make sure that people are paired up to each have some hands-on time with the equipment.

**TEXTBOX 10.3**

**ELEMENTS TO INCLUDE IN A GROUP TRAINING SESSION**

- Explanation of the specifications of the item
- Possible uses of the item
- Benefits of using the item
- Demonstration of how to use the item
- Hands-on experimentation with the item
- Details about the procedures for checking out the item
- Question-and-answer time
- Handouts with links to additional information from the website

### In-Space Workshops

Adding equipment or loanable technology training as an option in your library can be specifically about the services provided by your loanable technology program or it can be focused on a particular type of equipment or function (digital cameras, shooting video, basic editing). If you do not have a teaching area, you will need to set aside the equipment you will use, and you will need to reserve a couple of computers to demonstrate how to transfer files or use software related to the equipment so that the patrons can practice. You should be prepared for follow-up consultations that may be requested as patrons use the equipment and software. Here are some examples of libraries and technology departments that offer workshops:

- Case Western Reserve University: http://library.case.edu/ksl/freedmancenter/training/
- Georgetown University: http://www.library.georgetown.edu/gelardin/workshops
- Staffordshire University: http://www.staffs.ac.uk/support_depts/infoservices/it/catalogue/support/
- Tuscarora Intermediate Unit 11 regional educational service agency: https://www.tiu11.org/educational-technology/

## On-Location Workshops

Technology-training workshops can also be presented outside of the library. There are many reasons and benefits for holding a workshop in another location.

- If the library does not have the capacity to hold the number of anticipated attendees, partnering with others who do have the space can promote both the library and the partner (other departments, community venues).
- A classroom visit at schools and university settings is an excellent way to promote library services and to reach a larger number of students and faculty members with minimal time and effort needed on the instructor's part.
- It is easier for one presenter to travel to another location (such as for community outreach) than it is for the attendees to get to the library.

When offering a workshop on location, you will need to bring examples of the equipment offered in the loanable tech program and perhaps some laptops with software installed. Presentations that include images of the equipment are a good way to share information but do not compare to allowing others to see and try out the technology.

## Consultations

In the context of training, a consultation could be viewed as a less formal one-on-one patron help session. These help sessions can be scheduled by appointment or as a walk-up service provided by the library. If your department has plans to begin offering consultations by appointment, establish a general e-mail account (e.g., consultations@libraryX.edu) instead of referring patrons to a specific person's account. This has several benefits:

- Multiple people can check the account.
- It does not clutter one person's e-mail with requests.
- It is much easier to change account access if there is a change in personnel.

The type and extent of consultations that you provide will depend on your staffing expertise and available time. Many libraries may be able to offer basic training for patrons only on a walk-in basis, but then suggest to patrons that they set up a specific consultation time.

## Tours

Workshops and consultations are offered to assist in the education and troubleshooting of specific equipment, software, or technology-based topics and are usually conducted by someone with expertise or specific training. Tours, however, can be led by anyone in the library. You may want to script a segment to add to the general library tour that highlights the space, services, and equipment that the library offers. Ideally, you could provide this as a virtual tour so that it is broadly available and so that you can use it when you provide presentations and workshops away from the library. It is also a great marketing tool.

## Loanable Technology Specialists

Other individuals that need to be trained are any loanable technology specialists, who might not be part of the library, but might be community members willing to devote time to help as consultants or trainers with technology. Loanable technology specialists agree to spend a dedicated amount of time working with loanable technology each week, in the capacity of suggesting new technology items, doing advanced troubleshooting, processing new items, and even assisting with training others. The people who make up this group could be volunteers, student workers, part-time or full-time employees, or community members.

Ideally, at least one member of this group would be available whenever the library is open to serve as back-up support, even if it is to answer a question over the phone. Some of the support that they might offer would be to address specific patron inquiries about more advanced functions of the equipment or to help behind the scenes to prepare the technology for circulation. These individuals might also be responsible for upholding patron privacy concerns (for example, by deleting patron data from an item before it recirculates), keeping inventory up to date, or deciding which pieces should circulate with each item.

## Training Related to Support for the Program

Chapter 4, "Budgeting," discussed the importance of not overlooking the physical cost of continued support. However, there needs to be a designated person who is trained to oversee the budget, the planning, and the process of maintaining the equipment. Planning for ongoing support for library loanable technology is essential for a number of reasons:

- Many common loanable technology items have parts that can be purchased for far less than replacing the whole item.
- Minor technical support to handle fixes that do not require a large amount of time or expense can greatly lengthen the life of equipment, thus reducing replacement costs.
- Support of equipment can help in the overall understanding of how to use and educate others on the use of loanable technology. Exploring what broke, how it broke, and whether it is a common issue expands knowledge of the device's functions.

Outside of the cost of the equipment, your library loanable tech program will need an equipment-support person. Support, or maintenance and repair, could be done by a library staff member or by an external department or unit. If there is no library staff member with these skills, seek outside expertise or training so that at least one member of the library staff can provide this type of support for equipment. Most equipment websites have online customer service or even user forums that explain how to operate the equipment and fix common problems. Also, never underestimate the power of a search engine (e.g., Google) or user-submitted video sites (e.g., YouTube) when trying to learn more about different aspects of either the equipment purchased or potential purchases. The following section provides some examples of levels of support that your library may wish to use.

## Hierarchy of Support

There are different levels of support that are needed in a loanable technology program, and it is possible to train staff or students for those levels. This is useful because some technical support issues happen with great frequency or are relatively simple fixes that do not require skilled technical support to address.

**Desk worker.** Sometimes the support issue that is raised by a patron or discovered during check-in is simple enough or happens with enough frequency that the loanable tech desk worker has been trained to take care of the issue as it happens. A good example of this tier of support would be replacing batteries in a device (if the department is providing batteries) or helping a patron get data off of the equipment using the cables provided. Even with simple fixes that can be done directly at the desk, it is still a wise strategy to notify technical support via e-mail or some other tracking method. This allows tech support to be aware of frequently occurring issues. For example, if a part is constantly breaking on a specific piece of equipment, it may be beneficial, even if the fix is simple and low cost, to research alternative equipment or a different model number to reduce those issues in the future.

**Billing and technology support.** The next tier up deals with issues that are fairly easily solved but require the knowledge or intervention of another department to resolve. A great example of this would be replacing the memory card in a camera that was returned without one. In technical terms, this problem is easily solved by just replacing the memory card; however, the billing department may need to be notified so that the patron can be charged for the loss of the item.

**Higher-level technology support.** If staffing size allows for someone with specific technical-support experience, this individual may be able to identify and repair higher-level equipment support issues. Support of this level would generally involve an issue that requires taking apart a piece of equipment in order to replace a specific broken part and then reassembling that equipment. An example would be a tripod that has a broken crank arm. The tripod may have cost $120, but the parts (tripod-head replacement) needed to repair the tripod may cost only sixty dollars. Even if the replacement parts are not exactly the same model, it may be possible to use a combination of the old parts and the new parts to reconstruct a tripod for much less than it would cost to buy a replacement.

**Library technology support.** The final tier would involve a specific department dedicated to technical support. This could be staff who are certified to fix equipment that would otherwise require company replacement or warranty fixes. An example of this is someone who is an Apple-certified support technician or an HP-certified support technician. These people have the ability to fix laptops and other computer hardware instead of just directly replacing broken or faulty items.

## Key Points

With the advent of any new service in the library, it is important to plan for training staff and patrons. Marketing strategies can provide a subtle way of providing training and should be included in training efforts. This chapter has suggested various methods for training:

- Market through physical and social media
- Train every staff person who will work with the loanable technology how to operate and perform basic troubleshooting on the equipment
- Hold workshops and demonstrations for library users so that they can have some hands-on time with the equipment
- Make sure ongoing training is available for library staff and patrons

The next chapter will provide information on how to assess your program.

CHAPTER 11

# Assessing the Program

**IN THIS CHAPTER**

- ▷ Ways to use quantitative and qualitative methods to assess a loanable technology program
- ▷ Methods for evaluating usage of loanable technology
- ▷ Ways to gather patron feedback on their use patterns, needs, gaps, success stories, and suggestions for the program

THERE ARE A VARIETY OF tools that can be used to assess the effectiveness of a program, as well as to determine whether the program accomplished the intended goals. These include both quantitative and qualitative measures. A general assessment focusing on quantitative methods might use surveys, questionnaires, internal checks, usage statistics, or analysis of pre- and post-test results. Qualitative methods such as informal conversations, interviews, focus groups, and user comments can provide more in-depth information about what patrons are experiencing or what they desire. Evaluation can play both a formative role, helping to continually refine and update goals, objectives, and services; and a summative role, helping to ascertain whether the goals and objectives are being met. This chapter will provide some examples of tools that can be used to evaluate a loanable technology program.

## Determining the Questions to Ask

In order to assess a program, it is important to establish what you would like to know about the program. Are you interested in understanding if you met your goals and objectives for the program for the year? If your goal was to double the circulation statistics, that is easy to measure through available statistics from your library catalog system. If you want to measure how often patrons access a web page, you can use a web service like Google Analytics. However, if you want to measure satisfaction with the program or to gather feedback from patrons regarding the website, videos, training tutorials, programs, support, or equipment offered, you may benefit from using a variety of methods. Clearly, developing a good process and good questions is key. Some of the questions you might ask during an assessment or evaluation of a program include the following:

- Were the goals and outcomes accomplished? (Each goal or outcome will need to be listed as a separate question to explore.)
- Do patrons find the process of identifying which equipment is available intuitive? (This could include assessing the ease of using a website or library catalog.)
- Do patrons find the checkout and check-in process for equipment manageable?
- Are there adequate feedback opportunities pertaining to the program or process?

These questions can be answered through a variety of assessment methods that can be done individually with a patron or in groups. The questions can be posed face-to-face, online, on marker-board polls, on checkout forms, or at the service desk. The tools used may increase as your program grows. This chapter provides some options for gathering statistics for your program and then information for gathering more qualitative feedback.

## Quantitative Assessment Gathered Through Statistics

Tracking usage statistics (for a webpage, a learning guide, a tutorial, or a video) can be helpful in determining what resources individuals use and how they access those resources. Following are some examples of methods for tracking usage.

**Statistics available in the library catalog system.** If loanable technology has been cataloged, these statistics should be readily available. Make a spreadsheet to track usage over a given time period.

**Tours, training, classes.** This type of documentation of the number of staff-led sessions, including the number of participants, will help you understand the growth in interest in the program. It may be useful to track if these were staff-generated sessions or if they were requests from the participants. This could also help you understand how effective your promotion efforts are if there is an increase. If not, you might need to do more promotion and outreach for the program.

**Log-file analysis.** A log-file analysis could be used to detail users' activity on the web. These files can be illustrative in seeing how patrons search. If one goal was to assess whether the instructions for using a multisearch feature on the website were clear, the logs of the searches could be analyzed to see how successful users were. They could also be used to determine if users successfully created an account for a particular product or visited a particular web resource or database after going through a tutorial. The analysis could also track how users navigate to a particular resource, which may help you think about shortcuts to particular resources.

**Tracking new accounts.** Another method could include tracking new accounts. If a particular feature, such as getting to Lynda.com (to access software training), was emphasized, statistics for new accounts or evaluation of entry points for students going into Lynda.com during that time period could be tallied.

**Web page analytics.** Analytics, such as Google Analytics, can be used to evaluate web activity or determine how long users spend on a given web page or on entry or exit points to pages. If one of the goals was to get students to access video examples for using specific equipment, or to view training on particular software that is on a particular web page, the analytics could track entry points and patterns. They can also be used to track most-used pages, as well as underused pages (by looking at number of clicks to get there, time needed to complete the task, and whether a task was completed, such as viewing a tutorial). These results could be useful in redesign of the web page, as well as in promotion of resources. This type of measure can help determine if a goal has been met and can point to areas to focus on for improvement.

**Statistical tracking.** Most database and guide vendors offer a way to view statistics of database usage. These, along with internal tracking, could be useful to determine increase or decrease in training usage (if it occurs in a resource such as Lynda.com). Depending on the goal, you might want to determine if there was an increase or decrease in online guide or training activity after a library training session, tour, or class assignment. For example, if a tour or demonstration of loanable technology or media editing services is presented to a group, statistics could be gathered from some time before the session to a few weeks after the session to gauge if there was a marked increase in usage. Another example would be to document changes in equipment requests and checkouts following this session

## Qualitative Assessment Efforts

In addition to quantitative measures, it is useful to gather some qualitative feedback from patrons using questions to help solicit feedback. This can be done using informal and formal methods.

### Surveys and Questionnaires

Surveys and questionnaires are commonly used for assessment. They can be used to measure areas such as student satisfaction with equipment offered, training and support available, helpfulness of the staff, specifics related to the forms used, policies or procedures in place, how students use the equipment, or other suggestions. The results of these measures can be used to determine future direction of staffing, training, offerings, or the program in general. Surveys may measure the user's confidence (or awareness) in locating a specific piece of equipment or can be used to inquire about other equipment needed. These assessment techniques can provide an opportunity for the student to rate the program for relevance, ease of use, and satisfaction. When designing surveys and questionnaires, it is important to have colleagues review the questions and choices to make sure they are understandable and elicit the types of desired responses. A pilot or beta test with a small group of patrons should be conducted first to find other flaws. Then the survey can be administered either online or in print, depending on resources and the type of coverage desired. Some examples of survey questions can be found in chapter 2 and in appendix A.

An effective way to quickly gauge user feedback is to periodically post a "marker board" question where users can either publicly post their responses or put them in a prepared "ballot box." For example, you might pose a question such as:

- Do you still have a need to check out VHS players? Yes or No (This might help for decisions on how many VHS players to keep on hand.)
- Do you have equipment that can play Blu-rays? Or: What do you use to play Blu-rays? Nothing, Xbox, PlayStation, Blu-ray/DVD combo player (This may help you

decide whether to purchase Blu-ray players for circulation—as well as to figure out whether the library still needs to purchase DVDs along with Blu-rays.)

- Would you prefer that the library loan out iPads or tablets, and why?
- What one item do you wish the library would circulate?

Polls that consist of one or two questions can also be created and handed out at the service, information, and circulation desks as people wait to process their items. These questions, similar to the ones mentioned above, should be quick to answer, and patrons should be able to drop their responses in a box at the counter.

## Focus-Group Interviews

Another effective way to gather feedback is through focus groups. Effective focus groups typically consist of eight to ten participants. The facilitator uses scripted, broad questions that are not leading and asks them in each group. It is best to use a facilitator not involved with the project to ensure impartiality. It is also best to have two staff members per group: one can facilitate while the other records the responses. A useful technique is to project the notes on a large screen so participants can see the points and revisit them and add other comments.

Often, results from questionnaires are used as topics to be explored further in focus-group interviews. Patrons, students, and faculty can be invited to participate in a series of focus groups pertaining to specific questions. Responses can be valuable in helping to decide content, design, or other variables for a web page; equipment to offer, training needs (type, amount, and when offered), space needs, public equipment needs, and programming. If there is a prototype ready for viewing (a web page or policy, for example), a small group of patrons can be brought together to view and discuss the prototype (with scripted questions by the staff). The results of this evaluation can expand the staff's knowledge of the patrons' experience and their views on the design, content, usability and purpose of the web page, equipment, training, space, offerings, or procedures. This feedback can also lay the groundwork to improve and develop the learning environment. Chapter 2 provided some examples for setting up and conducting focus groups.

## Space-Design Focus Group

Another method for gaining feedback is to conduct a focus group that asks the participants to draw out what they envision for a space. In this case, it could be what they would like to see for an area that provides training and support for loanable technology and media editing. Participants are provided large blank sheets of paper and markers and asked to draw or write what they envision for the space. They need to consider what already exists and what they would like to see. They map out the space and display their renditions to the group along with a summary of what they envision. The evaluators later perform a content analysis and summarize the information for the library staff.

## Pilot (Beta) Test

Pilot testing should occur before publishing or making any item available. Focus groups can be used to test a web page, a training module, or a video. Others can also be solicited to provide feedback. Once the beta design is ready, it can be piloted with a few individuals or within a focus group to explore whether the design and content are accomplishing the goals and to test how intuitive the design is for users. This initial assessment can help determine if users can proceed without additional guidance. The initial assessment includes evaluator observations as well as user comments to correct any inadequacies in its design and content.

## Usability Testing

When developing web pages, training videos, or tutorials (such as for how to use equipment or editing software, for example), usability testing can be a compelling way to monitor effectiveness. Usability testing consists of testing a target population to determine how patrons interact with and progress through a web page or tutorial (or other guide or learning object) and asks patrons to provide feedback as they are observed performing tasks and exercises. Usability testing can reveal issues that are (or are not) important to users. It can also point out things that were left out that should not have been. Craven and Booth (2005, 190) suggest that these tests can illustrate users' opinions of a website, the usefulness of a service, the effectiveness of different search types and features, and "users' perception of the resource or service." The usability study, by focusing on summative as well as performance assessment, appears especially suited for measuring what users learn from a tutorial. The methods can also be useful in understanding, from a staff and patron's viewpoint, the process of checking out or checking in loanable technology.

### TEXTBOX 11.1

### GUIDELINES FOR USABILITY TESTING

Formal usability testing consists of observing and recording users carrying out specific requested tasks. Some fundamental guidelines recommended by Dickstein and Mills (2000) relating to the preparation and execution of formal usability testing are:

- Decide what to test.
- Design scenarios that will require the user to perform tasks you want to test.
- Write a script for administering the test to ensure consistency.
- Ask the testers to think aloud as they work through the tasks.
- Have a moderator/facilitator who asks questions.
- Have a recorder who transcribes what is observed (can be done with software).
- Identify individuals to act as testers who are representative of your target user population.
- Offer some kind of incentive for testers.
- Make sure you have a quiet, private place to do the testing.
- Record the test results as soon after the test as possible.
- Analyze the test results and recommend redesigns to correct problems identified.

Usability studies can be conducted in a variety of ways. The main focus is to listen to a user who is asked to go through a task, while encouraging additional feedback. It is best to record the session for later use. Following are some of the common methods used.

**Think-aloud protocol.** In addition to capturing movements and observations of a user working through usability testing, you can record user narratives during the process to gather valuable information. The use of a think-aloud protocol specifically reveals users' difficulties in the comprehension or use of a website or tutorial since their spontaneous comments reveal both the location and nature of any difficulty. For example, if a student says, "I can't figure out if I'm supposed to click on this word or not," the designer then knows to include more information to guide the user. The think-aloud process encourages participants to verbalize their thoughts, feelings, expectations, and decisions while interacting with the application (Dumas 2003). By "thinking aloud," or talking about what they are doing as they are doing it, participants reveal their thoughts as they complete each task, giving the staff member insight into why each action is being performed (Ericsson and Simon 1993). The participants' comments during the study may offer a source of data for individual assessment. Novotny and Cahy (2006, 158) noted that they provided a "richer set of information for analysis than simply recording keystrokes." According to Nielsen (1993, 19), "this additional insight into the user's thought process can help to pinpoint concrete interface elements that cause misunderstanding so they can be redesigned." This can help evaluators understand the reasons behind users' actions, and it can reveal misconceptions users might have about the system. Participants may feel uncomfortable talking through their actions and may need to be reminded periodically to "explain what you are doing" (to tell why they chose a selection, etc.).

The narration also helps if the evaluator is using use-of-time patterns, such as recording the time spent in navigation and reading screen information versus the time spent on actual learning activities. It can give clues as to why it took the participant extra time to choose something or reveal confusions based on language, organization, or design. In a study by Mestre (2010), the results indicated that students spent between forty-five seconds and three minutes to find a designated resource. Without the think-aloud process, the evaluators may never have known why or what students were thinking as they tried to figure out what to do next.

**Recordings.** Recordings (i.e., time log, video, audio, and eye-tracking data) can be used for triangulation with the data collected by the staff during the observed think-aloud protocol. A full repertoire of collected data might consist of a list of usability problems, quantitative data from logs, and qualitative data from the participants' verbal reports during each session, including any follow-up debriefing done with the participants (to ensure they had a chance to fully describe their experience).

**Patron debriefing.** Debriefing can be very useful during a usability study. Follow-up questions after each task of a usability study can be designed to help capture qualitative data. Questions can be asked to elicit whether or not the goals were met as well as to gain insight into adjustments that could be made. The qualitative data found in participants' explanations of their choices can assist in measuring the level of learning achieved through viewing the training tutorials, videos, guides, or web pages. Additionally, when the testing is finished, an overall debriefing of the pros and cons of the tutorial, video, or web page, with questions about what participants wish they had experienced or not experienced, can add additional information to future revisions.

**Individual interviews.** Individual interviews can be instructive, although they are very time consuming to conduct and transcribe. The number of participants needed will depend on the variables that are being tested and the target audiences involved. Conducting interviews or usability-study interviews with even a few individuals may help point out patterns, reactions, attitudes, difficulties, or concerns that would not be captured with other methods. Participants are able to more fully express why they approach a task in a particular way when they are allowed to freely verbalize a response.

## Broad Questions for Measuring the Effectiveness of a Web Page, Training Tutorial, or Video

When developing a resource, it is important to keep in mind that the audience may have different skill levels and approaches for using the resource than the developers do. The resource needs to be developed in a way that makes sense to the users, is easy for them to use, and provides the appropriate amount of content in a way that they can effectively navigate. Following are some broad questions that can be used with patrons to assess the resources.

**Is it intuitive and easy to use?** A vital question in assessing if a web page or guide or tutorial is effective is to determine whether the object is intuitive to use. Some of the key concerns that designers hope to assess are whether there are difficulties in navigation, whether the navigation is intuitive to users, and whether the navigation enhances the experience. In addition to checking whether the links and pop-up windows are reliable, evaluators may want to check on the ease of use of any practice exercises and quizzes. Additionally, they may target specific elements to see if users notice particular elements or features (such as images, descriptions, extra options, or an "Ask Us" link).

**Is the content appropriate?** Evaluators may want to target how well the content is presented. Is it too text-based, boring, or inappropriate for the target audience? User feedback in the form of a debriefing or through usability testing in which users verbalize their thoughts as they progress through a tutorial or web page can help highlight how appropriate the content is.

**Is the multimedia appropriate?** Tutorials can benefit from strategic multimedia applications to help accommodate various styles of learning, interactivity, and engagement. However, multimedia should be used only if it improves rather than distracts from the learning experience. Does the inclusion of a Flash object increase user interactivity, engagement, or comprehension? During usability studies, students will be able to voice their attitudes toward the value of any given multimedia application. It may also be possible to assess the value of applications by how well a student does with an exercise or question. If there are opportunities for users to pick and choose or manipulate objects, do they simply pick the first choice to keep things moving? Do they take the time to evaluate all the possibilities, or could the task have been accomplished without the use of Flash elements?

**Does it accomplish the intended goals?** During the design process of a web page, guide, tutorial, or video, its goals and objectives should have been identified. The goals should be specific, actionable, and realistic. The assessment of a tutorial should include ways to measure if these goals and objectives have been met. The outcomes may differ, depending on each participant's experience.

**TEXTBOX 11.2**

**TIPS FOR ASSESSMENT**

- Work with others to design your web page, tutorial, video, or guide. Decide which aspects are to be measured and their metrics (i.e., if the objectives in the tutorial or web page are clear, if the navigation is clear, etc.).
- Submit appropriate forms, if at an academic institution, for the institution's institutional review board (IRB).
- Formulate the documents required—these include the initial test plan, task list, information document for participants, checklist for test administrator, and pre- and post-test questionnaire to measure learner satisfaction and changes after participants go through the test.
- Create a plan for how participants will be recruited and how incentives will be funded.
- Pilot with a few participants and refine the test plan, task list, and information document based on the knowledge gained from the pilot.
- Conduct identical pre- and post-tests (regardless of target audience or if there is a control group).
- Conduct the main usability testing.
- Provide follow-up questions or do a debriefing.
- Analyze the results (coding responses).
- Write up results, draw conclusions, make recommendations, and revise.

## Assessment of Whether the Program Has Achieved Its Intended Goals

There are a number of tools and measures that can be used to assess whether the intended goals and objectives of a program have been met and whether they are specific, actionable, and realistic.

**Checklists, rating scales, and rubrics.** These methods evaluate how well the program and resources have met user needs. They allow staff to gather information and make judgments about what users know and do in relation to the established outcomes or goals. They offer ways of collecting data about specific behaviors, knowledge, and skills. Through collaboration with stakeholders in the community, especially targeting those who have used the services or directed others to use them, checklists could be distributed to patrons before they use the facilities or services. Then patrons could be asked to complete the checklist after using the services. The responses should indicate how well the program has met their needs. These could be similar to using pre- and posttests, but on a more informal level. Pre- and posttests can be used with the same users and can indicate if those users were better able to complete a task, process, or function as a result of a tutorial, service, or program.

**Evaluation of student work.** If the loanable technology program and equipment are made available to students for a class, it is possible to work with faculty to get feedback on the quality of the project. For example, many faculty members now require that students incorporate multimedia in a final project. Faculty could be asked to assess if the end product was of higher quality for students who took advantage of training related to media editing or used some of the equipment at the library (higher-end cameras, microphones, lighting, tripods) compared to students who did not take advantage of the equipment or training. This requires a liaison connection with faculty and a willingness on their part to have students indicate if they used any of the library resources and to communicate the results to the library staff. Although not immediate, this could provide evidence of how well the program has met its goals and objectives.

Assessment of a loanable technology program involves many aspects. It is important to go beyond the initial assessment done to create the program and to develop some type of usability assessment and outcomes assessment to determine if the program is accomplishing its intended goals. Ongoing assessment should be performed to ensure continued effectiveness, which will help in revisiting goals, outcomes, and needed promotion of the program. Outdated websites, tutorials, procedures, policies, and handouts could misinform and frustrate participants. Ideally, staff and users should review items periodically. Assessment can also help keep staff current on what patrons want and expect and whether there are any gaps in expectations and services. It is important to build in various assessment tools and measures that allow for internal assessment of products developed, an overall assessment of the program, and an assessment of whether the program has accomplished its goals and objectives. These assessments can help to fine-tune a program and to gather information that will inform the staff of changes to make so that they can achieve the stated (and envisioned) goals.

## Communicating Success Stories

It is also important to regularly communicate your results to your constituency and to highlight areas of growth, patron satisfaction, and decisions made based on user feedback so that the public understands the benefit of what you are providing. One of the best ways to promote a program is to highlight success stories by patrons. There are numerous ways to gather these, including by asking users to write a brief paragraph about how they used the equipment or service. These stories can be added to the library website, bulletin boards, and relevant newsletters about the library. You can also ask patrons to provide a link to the end product that can be added to the library's website. Another effective way to gather stories is to ask users if they would be willing to be part of a video to promote the service. You can provide a couple of questions to the patrons before the recording session. Statistical graphs can also be prepared to illustrate the growth in types of equipment being used and the number of training and information sessions conducted.

In addition to highlighting how the equipment and services are being used, you might also publicize suggestions made by patrons and any follow-up by the library. This can be done via a suggestion board (both physical and virtual) that indicates questions asked or suggestions given and how the library responded. This lets patrons know that you value their suggestions and also helps promote various aspects of the program if you indicate that as a result of patron requests additional tripods were purchased or that Go-Pro cameras are now available as a result of patron feedback.

If your library has developed a culture of assessment in which you practice ongoing assessment, these types of success stories will be easier to gather. It may take more time to communicate the results of your assessment and to prepare the statistics and success stories, but the effort can translate to more visibility for your program, which may help bring in additional funding, partners, and staff.

## Key Points

Assessment should be an integral part of a loanable technology program. It can help you understand if the goals and objectives are being met or if new goals or procedures need to be established. This chapter has included some of the methods that can be used to evaluate the program, along with ways to identify the successes, benefits, and gaps and the additional services, training, or resources needed. Regardless of method, some key points for assessment follow:

- Plan to do regular and iterative assessment of your program, including online resources, training, forms, policies, and procedures. Make the necessary revisions and changes so that you are providing an optimal service to your patrons.
- Seek out others to help with the planning and distribution of the assessments as well as to analyze and summarize the results.
- Regularly communicate your statistics and success stories to the public. It is a good way to promote the service and to validate the program's funding.

## References


Craven, Jenny, and Helen Booth. 2005. "Putting Awareness into Practice: Practical Steps for Conducting Usability Tests." *Library Review* 55, no. 3: 179–94.

Dickstein, Ruth, and Vicki Mills. 2000. "Usability Testing at the University of Arizona Library: How to Let Users In on the Design." *Information Technology and Libraries* 19, no. 3: 144–151.

Dumas, Joseph. S. 2003. "User-Based Evaluations." In *The Human-Computer Interaction Handbook: Fundamentals, Evolving Technologies and Emerging Applications*, edited by Julie. A. Jacko and Andrew Sears, 1093–117. Mahwah, NJ: Lawrence Erlbaum Associates.

Ericsson, K. Anders, and Herbert A. Simon. 1993. *Protocol Analysis: Verbal Reports as Data*. Denver, CO: Bradford Books.

Mestre, Lori S. 2010. "Matching Up Learning Styles with Learning Objects: What's Effective?" *Journal of Library Administration* 50, no. 7–8: 808–82.

Nielsen, Jakob. 1993. *Usability Engineering*. Freemont, CA: Nielson Norman Group.

Novotny, Eric, and Ellysa Stern Cahy. 2006. "If We Teach, Do They Learn? The Impact of Instruction on Online Catalog Search Strategies." *Portal: Libraries and the Academy* 6, no. 6: 155–67.

# Appendix A

# Stages of the Loanable Technology Program at the Undergraduate Library at the University of Illinois

THE UNDERGRADUATE LIBRARY at the University of Illinois at Urbana-Champaign (UIUC) began a loanable technology program to support the needs of students and faculty and allowed anyone with a valid UIUC ID to check out the equipment. The program supports the Undergraduate Library's mission and various library strategic initiatives (see http://www.library.illinois.edu/ugl/about/vision.html).

The Undergraduate Library clearly saw that an important part of the mission of the library was to provide support for classes, regardless of format. What began as an effort to provide some of the most frequently requested items (like graphing calculators) to students evolved over seven years to provide essentially anything that might be needed to create a multimodal project. Currently the library loans out 12 projectors, 15 pairs of headphones, 18 voice recorders, 21 tablets, 27 gaming items, 27 playback devices (iPods, MP3 players, DVD/Blu-ray players), 30 calculators (various types), 30 laptops, 43 chargers, 63 cameras (various models), 52 pieces of camera equipment, 70 data-storage devices, 74 adapters, and many other individual items. This is in addition to audio and video kits on reserve for various classes. For descriptions of the items, see http://www.library.illinois.edu/ugl/mc/loanable.html.

During the spring 2014 semester, these loanable technology items supported 301 individual classes, 84 different departments (44 percent of all campus departments), and many student organizations and groups.

In order to grow the program, the library staff worked with various stakeholders around campus to assess their needs and those of their students. Focus groups, interviews, and web surveys were conducted, both initially and at various points since (see Hahn et al. 2011; Mestre 2013). Most of the equipment is purchased through donor funds and campus library/information technology competitive funds, but items are purchased only if there is a direct correlation to need and they fit with the scope of our determined collection development policy. Chapters 3 and 7 describe this policy in more detail and chapter 4 outlines budgetary considerations. The program at UIUC is best discussed stage by stage, which might be similar to what other libraries experience as their program grows.

## Stages of UIUC's Loanable Technology Program

### Initial Stage

The loanable technology program at UIUC began as an outgrowth of a 2005 formal review that explored the creation of a "learning commons" space in the library, and was supplemented by funding provided by the Division of Intercollegiate Athletics to create a more robust undergraduate student space. The planning process included surveys, focus groups, informal interviews, and campus conversations with stakeholders to gather information on student needs (in particular technology needs) not being met with current resources. Analysis of the data led to the implementation of several new services and changes to existing services, including a restructuring of collections, spaces, and services in the Undergraduate Library and the establishment of a loanable technology program.

Based on ongoing assessments, items were prioritized and recommended for purchase, although some were deferred for a couple of years because of budget issues. Some of the tools were made available for checkout and some of the technology was located in a permanent setup in the library or through software installed on library iMacs. Items were purchased and processed in the following priority order:

- laptops
- digital cameras
- graphing and scientific calculators
- digital voice recorders
- portable devices such as MP3 players
- Apple computers for media production
- GPS units
- microphones
- scanners
- external hard drives
- portable projectors
- flat-screen monitors for study rooms

Figure A.1 illustrates some of the most popular loanable technology items that circulated during the first phase of the program, which are still popular today.

### Stage Two

Laptops and digital cameras formed the core of the initial loanable technology collection, which grew over time in response to assessment, student assignments, curricular changes, student requests, and other technology initiatives at the library. As more classes and

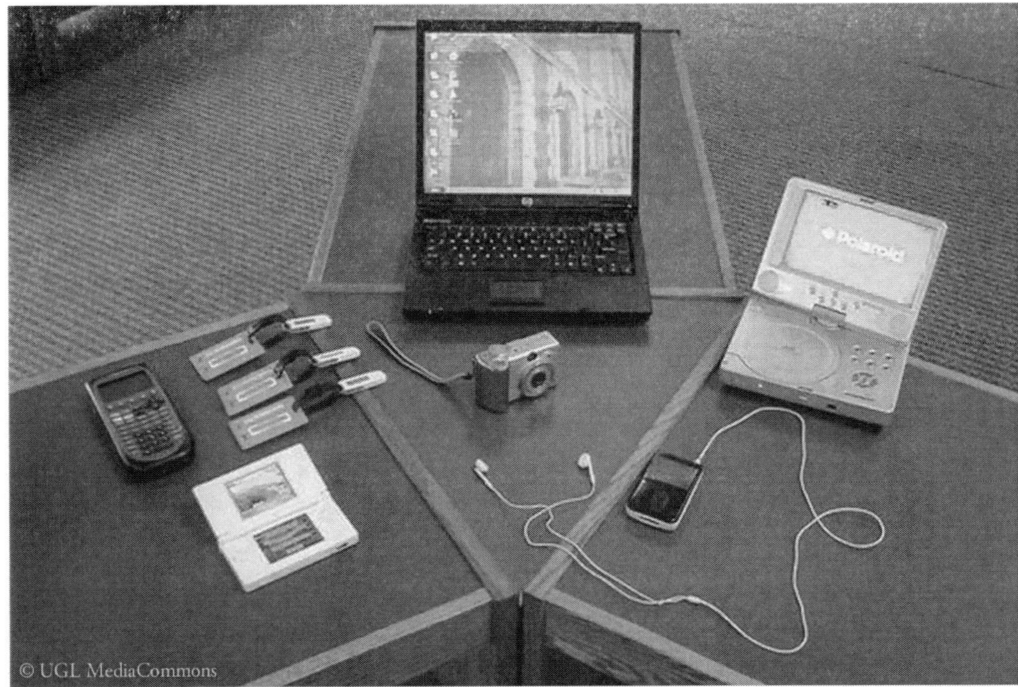

**Figure A.1.** Initial Stage of the Loanable Technology Program

instructors requested multiple copies of digital cameras and voice recorders, librarians worked with instructors to reserve these items. A staff member was assigned to track usage, to develop forms and a process for circulating the items, to review and recommend items for purchase, and to catalog and process the materials. The program grew considerably, which also led to having a separate loanable technology desk at the library. Figure A.2 illustrates equipment from phase two of the program.

**Figure A.2.** Second Stage of Loanable Technology Purchased

## Current Stage: Media Commons

The media commons, which opened in March 2013, integrated loanable technology into the services it offers. One of the goals of the media commons is to help create and support digital media, which requires available technology that students and faculty can check out. In response to this growing need, the loanable technology inventory has expanded to include basic and higher-end digital video cameras, digital video equipment, and other digital media creation tools. Items in the following categories were added to the inventory:

- HD digital cameras
- prosumer-level tripods ("prosumer" is the step between consumer and professional equipment)
- microphones and other audio-related accessories
- portable LED light kits
- audio and video kits

After seeing the popularity and demand of these digital media items, ideas were explored for ways to cover the increased demand while still keeping within the budget. One of the more popular ideas created, in conjunction with a group from central information-technology support, was the idea of a smartphone accessory kit, or "backpocket kit," which is illustrated in figure A.3.

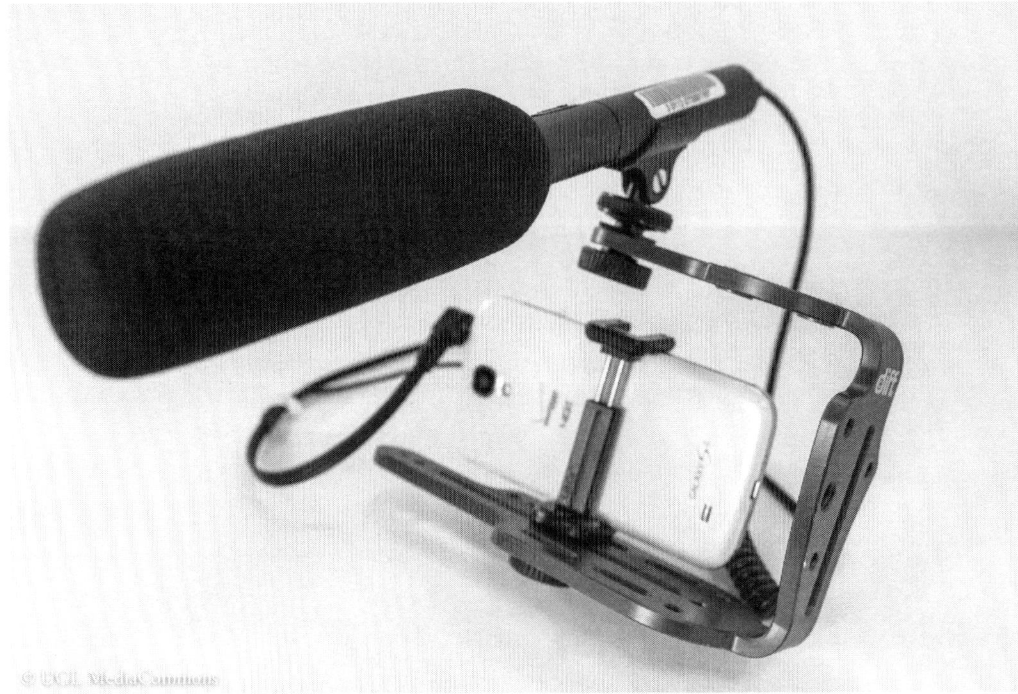

**Figure A.3.** Backpocket Kit with Smartphone

The idea of the backpocket kit is to promote the use of the video camera, digital still camera, and audio recorder that most users have in the form of a smartphone. Most current smartphones, regardless of manufacturer or operating system, have a competent camera for video and still images. What is usually lacking is the ability to record high-quality audio, as the microphone on the phone is small, omnidirectional, and usually far away from the subject of the recording. Because of this, many distracting environmental sounds are usually present in the recorded audio. Loanable technology provides a few accessories to enhance audio recording, which makes a smartphone readily usable for most digital media situations. At this stage in the loanable technology program, the staff and librarians are working more closely with faculty, students, and programs to understand what is needed, how to satisfy the need, and how to stretch the budget while still providing needed technology. The backpocket kits are examples of these efforts.

## The Library as Centralized Depository of Loanable Technology

The popularity of the loanable technology program, as well as the hours of availability and central service location of the library, led to the evolution of the library's role as a keeper and facilitator of other departments' or organizations' technology. Many other small collections of equipment were being purchased and distributed at different campus departments for class- or department-specific needs. Some of the challenges were making this equipment available for checkout, providing support for the equipment, and also making it easily accessible to its users. The current loanable technology program at the UIUC Undergraduate Library covers all those issues and thus becomes a natural, easy solution for other departments running into those issues.

In terms of service, the loanable technology program is working toward a more automated checkout process. Currently a form (a Word document) is filled out and most information is entered by hand at time of checkout. The goal is to use a web-based database that will automatically populate the form based on a couple of initial drop-down options. This will increase efficiency at the loanable technology desk and also potentially reduce human errors due to constant repetitive data entry.

The information above is provided as an example of how one academic library's loanable technology program evolved.

## References

Hahn, Jim, Lori S. Mestre, David H. Ward, and Susan Avery. 2011. "Technology on Demand: Implementing Loanable Technology Services in an Academic Library." *Library Hi Tech* 29, no. 1: 34–50.

Mestre, Lori S. 2013. "Media Commons: The Process and Value of Centralizing Services." *Library Hi Tech* 31, no. 4: 669–87. doi:10.1108/LHT-04-2013-0044.

# Appendix B

# Sample Surveys

THE FOLLOWING EXAMPLE SURVEYS can be used to assess technology and services. The first survey was provided both online and in print to assess patron use of and expectations for the media commons and the loanable technology service.

## Sample Survey 1: Revitalizing Services and Loanable Technology at the Media Commons

Thank you for participating in our survey. Your feedback is important. We will use information collected in this survey to improve the services and equipment available in the Undergraduate Library. Questions asking for your name or e-mail address are completely voluntary. You can discontinue this survey at any point.

1. Status:

   ___First year ___Sophomore ___Junior ___Senior ___Faculty ___Staff

   ___Graduate student ___Other (specify) _______________

2. Major: ______________________________________________

3. What are the **three** main reasons you chose a certain library?

   ___Café or vending machines

   ___Comfortable furniture

   ___Group study space

   ___Library help available

   ___Library resources I need

   ___Location

   ___Quiet space

___Reserve or media material

___Technology available

___Technology support available

___Wireless or electrical for my laptop and devices

4. Which of the following services have you used in the past year at a library? (Choose all that apply)

___Audio or digital voice recorder checkout

___Camera or video checkout (any kind)

___Device chargers or cables

___E-mail/Internet

___Game controllers, devices, or equipment

___Gaming center

___Flat-screen projection for laptops

___Group room checkout

___iPad/Kindle/Nook checkout

___Laptop checkout

___Media commons consultants

___Photocopy machines

___Projector checkout

___Research assistance

___Scanning equipment

___Technology support

___Video or audio editing software

___Video production studio

___Word/Excel/PowerPoint

___Writing assistance

___Other (specify) ____________________________________

5. What additional services **would you use** if they were included in the Undergraduate Library media commons? (Please list all that you would use) ____________________

__________________________________________________________

List options you want to learn about here: ________________________________

__________________________________________________________

6. What software do you need for your studies (or request your students to use)? Word, Excel, and PowerPoint are standard on computer terminals in the library. (Check as many as apply)

___AutoCAD

___Access

___Graphic-design software (please specify) ____________________________________

___Statistical software—please specify one of the following:

___ SAS ___SPSS ___Other (please specify) __________________________________

___Video/audio editing software

___After Effects ___Final Cut Pro ___Premiere ___InDesign

___Other (please specify)

___Web design (please specify) _____________________________________________

___None

___Other (specify) ___________________________________________________

7. Do you ever ask for software assistance from the consultants in the CITES labs or at the media commons support desk?

   ____yes ____no Comments________________________________

8. Do you ever ask for assistance at the information or reference desk at the library you use?

   ____yes ____no Comments____________________________________

9. Do you bring your own laptop to the library for your work? ____yes ____no
10. What time do you (or would you) prefer to use the library/media commons? (Choose your first choice)

    ___Before 9 a.m. ___9 a.m. to 5 p.m. ___5 p.m. to midnight

    ___Midnight to 6 a.m. ___Weekends

    ___Other Comments about time options ___________________

**Comments:**

________________________________________________________________

________________________________________________________________

________________________________________________________________

If you would like us to contact you about any of the information or suggestions that you have provided, please put your contact information below. Also, **if you would like to be entered for a raffle, please provide your e-mail.**

Name: ________________________________

___for raffle only ___for raffle and to contact me

E-mail: ________________________________

Thank you!

## Sample Survey 2: Excerpts from a Survey from Educational Technology

http://www.surveymonkey.com/s.aspx?sm=lSsWCYRNQ56LYjmZiaIuwA_3d_3d

Questions:

1. Department/agency/school/etc.
2. Rate overall skill with educational technology.
   a. Below basic
   b. Basic
   c. Proficient
   d. Advanced

3. Identify which of the following technologies you CURRENTLY USE. Mark all that apply. [Here you would list items that you currently have available or that others have requested you have.]
   a. Voice recorder
   b. Digital camera
   c. Digital camcorder
   d. Podcasting
   e. Scanner
   f. Graphing calculator
   g. Student-response system (clickers, etc.)
   h. Projector
   i. Etc.
4. Please indicate reasons/projects for using multimedia.
   a. Class assignment
   b. Videotaping a performance
   c. Etc.

# Index

# About the Authors

**Janelle Sander** manages the loanable technology program at the Undergraduate Library at the University of Illinois at Urbana-Champaign (UIUC). She has a BA in the teaching of English with a minor in school library media studies from the University of Northern Iowa and an MLIS from the University of Wisconsin–Milwaukee. Janelle has worked in a university archives, a K–12 library, and the interlibrary loan department at a small liberal-arts college. In her current role she is responsible for all aspects of the loanable technology program, including evaluation, selection, cataloging, processing, statistical tracking, training, billing, and the creation of documentation, policies, procedures, and best practices for the program.

**Dr. Lori S. Mestre** is professor of library administration and has been the head of the Undergraduate Library at UIUC since 2009. In addition to working with colleagues to keep the Undergraduate Library at the cutting edge of innovative services, she creates learning objects to help facilitate the research process. From 2005 to 2009, she was the digital-learning librarian at UIUC. Prior to 2005, Lori was at the University of Massachusetts–Amherst for nearly fifteen years, where she was the head of research and instructional services and previously the education librarian. In addition to her MALS degree, she has a doctorate in multicultural education. Her research and publications pertain to the intersection of online learning, accommodation of diverse learning styles, effective design that maximizes access to technology, and improvement of teaching practices regardless of platform. Recent research also focuses on the development and use of innovative technologies in libraries, including mobile applications and loanable technology. In addition to numerous articles on the above topics (see http://www.library.illinois.edu/people/bios/lmestre/), she has authored two previous books: *Serving Diverse Populations: Challenges and Opportunities* (2010) and *Designing Effective Library Tutorials: A Guide for Accommodating Multiple Learning Styles* (2012).

**Eric Kurt** is the media commons coordinator at UIUC. He has a BS and MS in computer graphics technology from Purdue University. Throughout college he worked for various institutions as an information technology support specialist. As a graduate student, he was a 3D computer graphics specialist for Simulex. After four years in industry, he returned to education as an instructor and taught computer technology at Indiana University-Purdue University Indianapolis and at the Art Institute of Indianapolis. He was promoted to academic department director of media arts and animation and web design at the Art Institute of Indianapolis. He has been the media commons coordinator at the Undergraduate Library at UIUC since 2012. He has presented and written on the media commons, media and video editing, loanable technology selection and use, and the value of collaborating with faculty to enhance technology support at libraries. An example blog post is available at http://webjunctionworks.org/il/blog/index.php/2013/06/03/media-commons-a-policy-for-providing-technology/.